TAKING WINGS AND WINNING

K.V. Subramaniam, President of Reliance Life Sciences (RLS), has devoted almost all of his thirty-five year long career to corporate business development; nurturing business opportunities in petrochemicals, energy, alternative energy, infrastructure, power, insurance, education, healthcare, agriculture and life sciences. The Reliance Life Sciences initiative, under the auspices of the USD 62 billion Reliance group in India, gave him a unique opportunity to create, ground-up, a research-driven business, addressing opportunities in medical biotechnology. K.V. Subramaniam is a chemical engineer from Madras University, a business management graduate from the Indian Institute of Management, Ahmedabad, a chartered financial analyst and a fellow of the Indian National Academy of Engineers. K.V. Subramaniam and his wife, a school teacher, live in Mumbai with his aged mother. They have a son who lives overseas.

TAKING WINGS AND WINNING

LEARNING FROM NURTURING A LIFE SCIENCES COMPANY FROM INCEPTION

K.V. SUBRAMANIAM

RUPA

Published by
Rupa Publications India Pvt. Ltd 2016
7/16, Ansari Road, Daryaganj
New Delhi 110002

Sales Centres:
Allahabad Bengaluru Chennai
Hyderabad Jaipur Kathmandu
Kolkata Mumbai

ISBN: 978-81-291-XXXX-X

First impression 2016

10 9 8 7 6 5 4 3 2 1

The moral right of the author has been asserted.

Printed by XXXXXX

I dedicate this book to:

My younger brother K.V. Srinivas. He met with an unfortunate accident on a soccer field in the Indian Institute of Management, Ahmedabad, on 28 January 1987. After over five years in a coma and several surgeries, his life came to a tragic end in 1992. My brother was a peaceful and pensive individual, whose brilliant academic career and life was cut short at the young age of thirty.

My father, K.S.V. Subramaniam, who was constantly at Srinivas's bedside and nursed him meticulously and with total dedication, only to join him less than two months after his demise, in the world beyond.

My mother, P.S. Subbalakshmy, who provided every support she could in nursing Srinivas. And resolutely endures, to this day, the tragic loss of her son and husband within a span of two months.

Their lives teach me to take success with self-effacement and setbacks with serenity, while striving to move ahead.

Contents

PROLOGUE

'Founders can ill-afford to fear failings.'

Reliance is one of the fastest growing companies in the business world. The US$ 62 billion India-based global conglomerate has been built in over two generations and less than four decades. The mere mention of Reliance evokes strong responses—both admiration and apprehension: admiration for its business initiatives that have an expansive and accelerated format and apprehension for its ability to radically alter the competitive landscape. How does Reliance build businesses with such rapidity in related and alien sectors? This has been a mystery to most people.

This book is my first-hand account of a new business taking shape in the Reliance group. I was formally schooled in chemical engineering, business management and financial analysis. I spent thirteen years in IPCL before I joined Reliance in corporate business development in 1994, long before Reliance acquired IPCL in the year 2002. I have spent twenty-two years in Reliance working across several industry sectors. My long tenure is not unusual within the company for many in leadership positions, but one that triggers a sense of disbelief in others outside Reliance.

I was not schooled in biology or medicine. But despite this, I was given a mandate by Mukesh Ambani to build from scratch a research-driven, biotechnology business—Reliance Life Sciences—a relatively new, microscopic, and people-driven business.

I have attempted to bring to this book my experiences, interactions, learning and frustrations in shaping Reliance Life Sciences. This book portrays the blossoming of this non-linear, complex and long-haul business from a developing country, on to the global stage, in a graduated manner, which is in sharp contrast to the evolution of its global commodity-driven, linear parent company, Reliance Industries Limited.

In portraying each stage of the evolution of Reliance Life Sciences, I have adopted a format of presenting germinal aspects first in every chapter, which is followed by their amplification in later chapters with touch points from scientific, technological, sociological, cultural, economic, psychological and, even, spiritual angles. I have intertwined the narrative with experiences from my life, because Reliance Life Sciences is integral to my psyche. The title comes from my fascination for aerospace.

The narration is neither about the application of management theories nor about prescriptions. However, inferences can be made by the reader, from some insights into the 'Reliance way' or from the pitfalls and challenges in building a new business. The Reliance name does not imply that the company is piggybacking on the Reliance group. Reliance Life Sciences has had to earn its own bread, after an initial incubation period and gradually was given greater degrees of latitude from the parent company, consistent with its growth and profitability. That's the way successful businesses in the Reliance group are built.

In Reliance, success is measured most by cash profits—instead of just by revenues or gross profits—and least of all by market capitalization. Achievements matter more than efforts. It took significant effort for Reliance Life Sciences to reach, from scratch, its first one hundred million dollars in revenues—

where it is currently placed. Growing beyond this will be seen as milestones on the path to expansiveness.

Reliance Life Sciences has ventured into areas that very well-endowed pharmaceutical companies in India have either avoided, or tried out and given up. In the process, Reliance Life Sciences has developed, and continues to develop, several differentiated biotechnology-based medical products and services of value. These products and services address the unmet medical needs of patients in India and other parts of the world.

In my view, this book would be useful to budding and potential entrepreneurs, as well as students of management. The biotechnology industry context is just a backdrop; the essence is about the generic aspects of entrepreneurship, in building a successful new hi-tech business from scratch. Aspects related to building and managing a technology organization would make sense in many industry and business settings.

PART A

Intuitive Nurturing

1

LOCATING THE LARGER SOCIAL PURPOSE

'Blessed are businesses that serve
an underlying social purpose.'

Way back in business school, I had learnt that business is about profitable exploitation of opportunities. But, to me, at a deeper level, a meaningful business is really about meeting the unmet needs of society in a harmonious way. Some of us used to tease our business school batchmates scrambling to secure jobs with transnational, fast moving consumer product companies. We would say, 'At the end of your career, what will you tell your grandchildren? "Instead of a red soap, I sold a blue soap?"'

At one level, locating the larger social purpose for a new business can be based on spending time and effort in meticulously understanding societal needs and imperatives; in local, regional, national or global settings. At another level, it can come about from deep-rooted experiences and sufferings in one's own life and that of near and dear ones. These aspects will translate into a business proposition only when entrepreneurial energies emerge, either within oneself or facilitated by the family or business environment.

It is not that businesses which begin by addressing

societal needs that are fully met will not be worth pursuing.
In such situations, there has to be a compelling case, long-
term competitive advantage and sustainability.

OVERTURE

In November 2001, I was told by Mukesh Ambani to look
at biotechnology as a new business opportunity. It was his
intuition that probably led him to target biotechnology as a
business opportunity of the twenty-first century. He was clear
that even if biotechnology was to ultimately undermine the
existing businesses of Reliance, he wanted to proceed with it.
To him, this represented creative destruction. This could have
been possible with biopolymers replacing thermoplastics and
biofuels replacing conventional hydrocarbon fuels, through
the domain of industrial biotechnology. Both these domains
continue to be the holy grail of biotechnology, even today. The
Indian pharmaceutical industry had left some flanks open and
biotechnology was one of them. Here was an opportunity. I
started in right earnest to understand biology, biotechnology
and medicine.

REMINISCENCE

In my quest for knowledge, I visited hospitals and talked to
doctors. It was here that the real purpose of this business
that I was embarking on hit me hard in the face—that I was
connecting my new engagement with my past experience. A
terrible health-related experience that my family had undergone
came back to me, not in the form of memories, but as a stark
reality of life that added meaning to my engagement with
biotechnology, medicine and life sciences.

My family had gone through several traumatic years because
of an unfortunate and freakish accident that my younger
brother, K.V. Srinivas, had on the soccer field on 28 January

1987. It was exactly a week before my wedding. Srinivas was academically brilliant and was a sportsman as well. He was a National Science Talent scholar and among the top-ranked in his year in the intensively competitive entrance examinations of the Indian Institutes of Technology (IIT).

Srinivas chose to study mechanical engineering at IIT, Madras. He went on to be the sports secretary at the institute, captained the volleyball team, and played in the football and basketball teams. After graduation, Srinivas did not want to go overseas for higher education as was the norm among the IITians. He did not want to burden my father, who had by then, retired. Instead, Srinivas worked at Tata Motors in Pune for two years as a graduate engineer trainee, and then joined IIM, Ahmedabad in 1986. At IIM, he joined the soccer team and was a goalkeeper. He had a tragic accident on the soccer field, which was the beginning of his long drawn-out encounter with death.

MEDICAL DISTRESS

On the evening of 28 January 1987, while diving to save a goal, he was hit on the left temple area of his head by the shoes of his team's full back and a fellow batch mate. Srinivas collapsed on the field with blood oozing out of his nose and fluid leaking from his ears. He had a severe brain injury with several fractures in the left temporal area of his skull.

Srinivas was hospitalized for over eight months, first in V.S. Hospital in Ahmedabad, then in Dr Thakkar's nursing home in the same city. Later, he was shifted to a leading multi-specialty hospital in Mumbai. Here, he was under the care of a nationally eminent neurologist. He developed meningitis (infection of the brain) immediately after a craniotomy (brain surgery) performed by a neurosurgeon to remove a septic cyst caused by infection. He had developed the infection during the initial hospitalization in Ahmedabad. Antibiotics could not deal with the infection and he had unabated high fever of over 105° F.

Srinivas went into a delirious state, developed ventriculitis and eventually slipped into a coma. Little by little, the grey matter of his brain was destroyed and dissolved in the cerebrospinal fluid, which got discharged through the spinal cord into the abdominal cavity. This life threatening condition due to infection deep within the ventricles of the brain was irreversible.

Srinivas had two cranial shunt surgeries. These surgeries were carried out to address the problem of the cerebrospinal fluid becoming thick with the dissolved grey matter, which raised the intracranial pressure. The surgeries involved bypassing the flow of cerebrospinal fluid through a thin plastic tube running under the skin, from the lower side of the brain, all the way to the abdominal cavity. Another craniotomy was done to fix an 'omaya reservoir' in a hole drilled into the brain, through which antibiotics could be injected directly into the brain.

A tracheostomy in the throat was done to make a hole to hook a ventilator for the long term, as he could not breathe on his own. Srinivas also had innumerable spinal punctures to draw out cerebrospinal fluid for testing. To compound matters, Srinivas developed large bedsores on his lower back due to nursing negligence in the hospital.

BRUTALITY OF HEALTHCARE

Srinivas bore the brunt of the brutality that exists in the healthcare industry. Untrained doctors caused him pain when they punctured the spinal cord to take a sample of cerebrospinal fluid. I vividly remember an untrained neurologist at the multi-specialty hospital, trying a few times unsuccessfully, to puncture Srinivas' spinal cord, causing Srinivas to scream during his state of delirium. All I could hear while standing outside his hospital room were his repeated screams of: 'This doctor is a fraud.' These were Srinivas's last words.

At that time, we did not realize the reasons for, and the meaning of, what he said. Much later, as my understanding of medicine grew, I realized that the neurologist did not have the experience to draw out cerebrospinal fluid. He was using Srinivas to hone his skills. He also tried to draw cerebrospinal fluid from Srinivas's right temple. We realized later that such a procedure could have led to the suspension of the neurologist's medical registration in other countries where a doctor or a surgeon is expected to conform to defined and documented standards of care. Through our tragic experience emanating from Srinivas's accident, we gained a deeper understanding of a patient's suffering, the travails of near and dear ones, and the brutality of the healthcare system.

I vividly remember the crass insensitivity of one doctor in the intensive care unit who asked us, 'How long do you expect us to keep the ventilator on for Srinivas?' Or of another insensitive cardiothoracic surgeon who did not even care to stop and address the concerns of another patient's paranoid wife who was running after him in the hospital corridor to enquire about a pacemaker to be implanted in her husband. The cardiothoracic surgeon retorted, while he continued to walk without looking back at her: 'Have you arranged for the money?' Receiving an affirmative answer, he pronounced, 'In that case, I'll do it tomorrow.' Money seemed to matter more to him than the patient and his family. It is ironical that every Indian currency note has a picture of a smiling Mahatma Gandhi, when there are such crass violations of the lofty principles that Gandhi stood for and practised. These violations take place with pedestrian frequency in Indian society.

To the hospital's credit, there were many other doctors who were large-hearted and had a humanitarian approach. Their goodness prevailed. Srinivas continued on a ventilator till he managed to breathe on his own.

BETWEEN LIFE AND DEATH

Srinivas did not have any health insurance since he was not covered by my father who had retired from his employment a few years earlier, and neither did he qualify as a dependent at my brother's company or at my company. Early on, in the course of his treatment, after all the family savings had been exhausted, he was shifted to a 'concessional' ward. Here, we had to pay a small percentage of the charges, thanks to a medical trust. We were often asked to buy certain medicines and medical devices that were written out as prescriptions. Sometimes, these requirements came in the dead of night. Either my brother or I would have to go out in the middle of the night, prescription and cash in hand, looking for a twenty-four hour chemist. We had the constant fear that any delay in getting the medicine or its non-availability could compromise Srinivas's extremely fragile condition.

Even though our family had exhausted all its financial resources, we still had the will to do everything we could to bring Srinivas back to life, even if he was going to be handicapped for the rest of his life.

Srinivas was finally discharged in a vegetative comatose state. We moved him in this state by train from Mumbai to our parents' home in Hyderabad. He continued in the same state for over five years. He was nursed with intense devotion by my father, who stopped praying to God. He used to say that the only temple for him was Srinivas. On weekends or at every conceivable opportunity, my brother and I would relieve our father from the demands of caring for Srinivas, even if it involved travel at short notice from Baroda or Mumbai, by train or bus, often in unreserved and jam-packed railway compartments.

After five years in a deep unconscious state, during which he traversed a very slow and irreversible pathway to death, Srinivas had an attack of pneumonia due to his immune-compromised state. He died on 16 July 1992 on the way to a local hospital in Hyderabad.

Within two months of Srinivas's demise, my father died of an undiagnosed and unexplained aggressive ailment in a hospital in Hyderabad. It was suspected to be malignant ascites in the abdomen. The cause of his ailment could well have been extreme depression or a broken heart. He spent just one week in the hospital before his death.

My father had donated Srinivas's eyes to the L.V. Prasad Eye Hospital and Research Centre in Hyderabad and we decided to donate our father's eyes to the same centre. There is a small sense, deep down, that probably someone, somewhere is seeing the world through the eyes of Srinivas and of our father.

COMATOSE MEDICINE

Those long years of caring for Srinivas and spending time in hospitals, showed me the unpleasant side of medicine, how some medical practitioners were trapped in time and resorted to outdated practices while, others, though being up to date, were highly self-opinionated and formed 'barriers' to those outside themselves. I also learnt a lot about the reactive nature of medicine, how it responded to situations as they surfaced and how many doctors and hospitals fleeced patients. Even mortuary assistants, hearse drivers, staff and policemen exploited the vulnerable in the event of death, accidents and post-mortems. In a sense, the practice of medicine was comatose for us in the family.

Dealing with a comatose patient taught me that the human brain is the least understood and explored of all human body organs, and showed me the straitjacketed way in which psychiatrists deal with mental disorders. These medical practitioners have a limited idea about the brain and behaviour, and mostly turn their attention to a few biochemicals, such as serotonin, adrenaline and melatonin, which rise or fall based on internal or external stimuli.

I experienced first-hand, medical care related to the brain when in March 2013 I suffered a head injury due to a fall in a hospital bathroom. I had a close shave with death and was in delicate health for six months. During this period, I continued to be engaged with building Reliance Life Sciences and opted for deep breathing and music as the therapies to help me recover.

DESTINY IN BIOTECHNOLOGY

By sheer coincidence, or due to the machinations of a higher power, both my twin brother and I found our divergent careers converging into biotechnology. I joined Reliance Life Sciences Private Limited at the pinnacle of my career in corporate business development, and he joined Indian Immunologicals Limited. Today, this accomplishment gives us a great sense of satisfaction; not from a patriotic perspective but from the perspective of self-actualization. Imagine a chemical engineer and a mechanical engineer heading two biotechnology companies; one in biotherapeutics and the other in health vaccines. It was clearly not by desire or design. Biotechnology was my destiny.

When I graduated in chemical engineering in 1979, I wanted to pursue higher education and a career in India. So did my twin brother who graduated in mechanical engineering the same year. Despite being among the top rankers at university, we wanted to remain in India and did not want to be second-class citizens in a foreign land. We also believed that we had benefited from a subsidized government education in India, and wanted to give back to Indian society in our own way. Hence, both of us proceeded to study business management at the Indian Institute of Management, Ahmedabad. In contrast, many of our engineering batchmates saw opportunities in higher education abroad. About half of my graduating class left for the United

States of America. Most of them have since been working as faculty in US universities or as senior research scientists in global research and development laboratories.

We never took the GRE, GMAT or TOEFL tests that were necessary to gain admission into US universities. We just watched, with some amusement, how our batchmates chased applications, took tests, sought recommendations from professors, and then waited eagerly for an acceptance letter. When they received it, they would run down the corridor of the hostel yelling and announcing their selection. At other times, they quietly withdrew into their rooms to brood in privacy.

DESTINY IN INDIA

Ancient Sanskrit texts refer to India as a land of milk and honey. Modern scholars describe it as a land of opportunities, more so as one of missed opportunities. Since historical times, India has been taken advantage of, first by the rulers of the erstwhile princely states, then by the Mughals, followed by the British and, since independence, by many among the privileged class. However, my brother and I found that our conviction in the future of India was vindicated. The country has provided us the opportunity of being first-class citizens.

In a larger context, the Reliance group represents Indian aspirations. 'What is good for India is good for Reliance', is the common refrain within the Reliance group. Some opportunities are obvious, as with energy and materials. Others have to be sniffed out, as with biotechnology, communications and information technology. The challenge is in finding and capitalizing on opportunities which strike the right balance between lower prices and higher volumes.

Around the turn of the century, the seeds of an information and communications business were being sown in Reliance. This later led to a successful business, manifested by Reliance Infocomm Limited (now Reliance Communications Limited).

The vision of the Founder Chairman Dhirubhai Ambani, an icon for business in India, was to deliver a phone call at less than one US cent a minute. At that time, the incumbent operators in India were charging users thirty times more. This vision fundamentally propelled India to become one of the foremost and lowest cost mobile telephony markets in the world. Today, Reliance Jio Limited is building on this achievement with a fourth generation wireless broadband initiative, which is blanketing every nook and corner of India with immersive content in education, health, media, and entertainment and transaction services.

DESTINY FOR LIFE SCIENCES

In life sciences, the focus is on meeting the unmet medical needs of patients through novel, high-quality and cost-competitive medicines. It is also about addressing uncared-for disorders and diseases and mitigating patient suffering. This requires research, product development and clinical development in disease domains that are too small or of no concern to the developed world. Historically, many big pharmaceutical companies have refrained from taking advantage of the extensive opportunities in life sciences in the developing world. Reliance Life Sciences has taken advantage of some of these opportunities and plans to be engaged with them for the long term.

Every medicine that is developed or cost-engineered can become a potential opportunity for every person inhabiting this planet. At one level, the prosperity of the pharmaceutical industry rises with the misery of humanity. At another level, it contributes to alleviating human miseries. Irony could not have found a better playground.

Innovation in medicine is not just about finding cures for diseases, but also about making drugs competitive, accessible and affordable. Innovation can also make the health delivery system more efficient. If the 'comatose' healthcare system has to wake up, there must be an awakening of all the players—policy planners, pharmaceutical companies, hospitals, doctors, paramedical staff and, above all, government officials.

Thus, in life sciences, the higher the cost-effectiveness and accessibility of products and services, the stronger is its social purpose. The greater the concern for patient interests, instead of patents and profits, the deeper is its societal support. Herein lies its destiny.

DESTINY WITH A LARGER SOCIAL PURPOSE

Biotechnology thus provided both the Reliance group and me, the stage for a larger social purpose. The Reliance group had the opportunity to engage with a new technology sector that could potentially undermine its core businesses of polyesters, polymers and chemicals, but could also contribute to alleviating patients' suffering. In hindsight, I realized that Mukesh Ambani had provided me with the opportunity to steer an engagement in this space with fervor.

2

INITIATING DEVELOPMENT

'New businesses would do well to first fathom
and then fire-up.'

The buy-in process for a new business opportunity can get complicated, and, at times, very demanding. In a conglomerate, a new business proposal has to compete with incumbent and other new business opportunities on returns on capital employed. For startups the competition is from other investment opportunities that are part of the 'deal flow' of angel investors, venture capital firms and investment banks. For the head of a new business or an entrepreneur, their own situation is everything. But for the investor, the same situation is one among several options. In such a milieu, an outstanding opportunity generates interest. But beyond interest, there must be depth and expanse to convert interest into investment.

Therefore, for any new business, beginnings are critical. Clarity of thinking, the big picture, long-term competitiveness, scalability and, with many investors, social impact, matter, particularly for new businesses in less understood or evolving domains.

A business plan is a product of intuition, insight and

intention. It is neither fluid nor cast in stone. It has to be dynamic, as new information, developments and analysis emerge. In businesses where imponderables abound, a starting point can be a development plan that evolves into a business plan. This approach limits the investor set to those who are development-driven as against those who are transaction-driven.

DEVELOPMENT PLAN

In the Reliance system, a group of key decision-makers form the Executive Council. The council is comprised of Mukesh Ambani, full-time directors on the board, and heads of key corporate functions—technology, projects, finance, treasury, human resources and management information systems. Decisions of strategic importance are taken at weekly council meetings. Decisions are based on consensus, in most cases, among the internal stakeholders. Input from external well-wishers is also factored in, based on the context.

Biotechnology was undoubtedly a risky business for Reliance. It was not for the faint-hearted. It was complex, therefore it was better to dabble in it first, get a feel for the terrain, and then step up on scale. The journey was going to be a long one, and it would take time to realize the fruits or rewards for our efforts. Therefore, I believed a development plan was more useful than a business plan in the company's evolutionary phase. There was pressure from the Reliance system to write a business plan and not a development plan. But for me, writing a development plan was the priority.

Some people believed that I was given too much freedom to make choices of this kind. This did not bother me, but endowed me with a sense of responsibility. I had to be sure of what I was doing. Fortunately for me, Mukesh Ambani consented to my request. His trust and confidence mattered most to me.

So I got down to looking at the biotechnology opportunity in some detail. I was schooled in corporate business development and had spent many years across sectors ranging from petrochemicals, to petroleum refining, infrastructure, insurance, alternative energy, agriculture, and education. With such a broad span of engagement, initially, I had a sense that the new engagement with biotechnology was going to be relatively easy.

But biotechnology was not easy, to say the least. Not having studied biology seemed a serious handicap. So, I read every book and article on biotechnology that I could lay my hands on, as well as a large number of research and industry reports. The Scripps reports were particularly useful. By interacting with subject experts and even reading school textbooks, I gained valuable insights into this nascent field.

Dr Vishwas Sarangdhar and Dr Jacqueline Dias, who came on board early on, as consultants, also helped me understand biotechnology, as did visits to several Indian research institutions in India and overseas. As a neophyte in the biotechnology industry, I was in a learning mode at that time, and continue to be a keen learner even today.

My study helped me realize that if anyone claims to be a biotechnology expert, he or she is eon years away from the truth. Biotechnology is unfathomable; the process of studying it is much like sitting on a terrace, gazing at the clear sky on a starry night and trying to unravel the mysteries of the universe.

There are many imponderables in biotechnology, more than what is evident or apparent. For every biotechnology company that has made the grade, many have fallen by the wayside. Patents matter much less than know-how. Drug discovery is no different from oil and gas exploration, from a probability theory point of view. Manufacturing plasma proteins is basically not very different from fractionating and purifying crude oil in petroleum refining. Both involve separating valuable fractions and molecules through biochemical or chemical processes.

DEVELOPING A GAME PLAN

During a break from work, while I was in Hyderabad visiting my parents in January 2001, I wrote the development plan. The plan addressed opportunities in therapeutics at a conceptual level. Nowhere did it say anything about the means, manner and mode of money-making in the business. Imagine a business manager working in a company characterized by a hard-nosed commodity business environment and thought processes.

I followed this by preparing a document for review. It revolved around starting small in all the three areas—medical, plant and industrial biotechnology. The proposition was that, at some stage in our evolution, we could evaluate what made sense and then scale up. This was a radical departure from the traditional Reliance practice of conceiving a business on an expansive format, getting the long-term competitive advantage right, putting the might of resources behind the business and working on meticulous execution on the ground.

BUY-IN

'Let's present this to DHA,' Mukesh Ambani said, referring to the late Founder-Chairman Dhirubhai Ambani. In Reliance, titles are for the external world. Internally, we are known by our initials or first names. It did not matter if you were a president or a manager. What mattered was the value you brought to the organization. This value which we call CMV or current market value, is not constant. Your value can change from day to day, like indices in equity or commodity markets.

Making a presentation to DHA was a tradition in Reliance. All new business and strategic aspects would be presented to DHA for his blessings. A partial paralytic stroke had restricted

DHA's activities in the office. He would only be available for a few hours every day. However, this did not take away his ability to be a great listener. He would listen very intently without interrupting the presenter and would then ask a question or two to seek clarifications. After that he would pronounce his judgement.

DHA had a way of looking at issues from an angle that others may not have considered. He invariably caught business leaders off guard and exposed them for not thinking matters through sufficiently. In some rare cases, he would pronounce 'a go, no go' verdict. Then an entire team's continuation in Reliance would come under a cloud. Making a new business presentation to DHA was akin to the devout going to a place of worship to seek God's benevolence, and coming back with more to think about, or empty-handed.

I did witness, from close quarters, the way DHA's mind worked. In 1995, the liquefied petroleum gas marketing strategy of the world's largest petroleum refinery being set up at Jamnagar, was being presented to DHA. The differential strategy was to have every neighbourhood store, or *kirana* shop as they are known in India, stock up to eight LPG cylinders (permissible under the Indian Explosives Act). DHA listened intently to the presentation and wanted to know how much the shopkeeper would make by stocking and selling Reliance LPG cylinders. The figure was of the order of Rs 2,000 per month (US$ 40 per month at that time). 'Forget about it and think differently,' was his pronouncement. The experts in the room, both from India and overseas, were left dumbfounded.

On another occasion, the bidding strategy for fourteen oil and gas exploration projects opened by the Indian government for private participation, was presented by a team. This team consisted of business, geophysical and geological experts hired by Reliance. They had studied all the blocks extensively, and suggested three blocks to bid based on the reservoir potential. DHA asked a simple question, 'How much more would it cost to drill in deep sea if one bid for all the fourteen blocks on offer?' The answer was that it would cost marginally higher. 'Go and bid for all the fourteen. This is no-brainer,' he exclaimed. The rest is history. Reliance won all the blocks and created one of its largest businesses. DHA's simple logic was that the cost for bidding for all the blocks was incremental compared to the cost for just three blocks. In any case, striking oil or gas in the context of three, or all, depended on the probability of success.

SEAL OF APPROVAL

So here I was in March 2001, a rank outsider to the industry, standing in front of DHA in his spacious, all-white, and uncluttered office talking about the proposed life sciences initiative. Dr Vishwas Sarangdhar's presence in the room was comforting. The deal was that I would make the presentation and Vishwas would answer all the technical questions.

I was not nervous since I had interacted with DHA on previous occasions—such as reading sessions with him in the office and at his house—and knew what the outcome would be. One such experience pertained to the chairman's address for the Reliance shareholders' annual general meeting. The annual general meeting is traditionally a congregation of thousands out of the 2.4 million equity shareholders of Reliance Industries Limited. It was the most important day on DHA's annual calendar. He would prepare extensively for this event. A few colleagues from other disciplines and I would go to his home a few evenings before the event to practise our speeches. He would make me read my speech and suggest changes. Then DHA would practise it until he got the delivery right. With others, he would predict the questions that would come up and prepare the responses. His attention to detail was exemplary.

As the presentation on the life sciences opportunity and plan progressed, I noticed the childlike excitement on DHA's face. This was especially evident when the subject of stem cell therapies and competitive products that could address the global needs of patients came up. Mukesh Ambani would step in from time to time to amplify a concept. DHA listened intently and then finally pronounced, 'We must do this.' After the green signal from him, the life sciences initiative was signed, sealed and delivered.

Ironically, it was no occasion to celebrate. On the contrary it was a relief, as well as a great responsibility resting on my shoulders, as well as the shoulders of the members of the small nucleus team of Reliance Life Sciences. I knew what was coming next—a demand for an implementation plan.

DARE TO SPEND

As anticipated, after we stepped out of the room, Mukesh Ambani promptly said, 'Let's work on an implementation plan. Do you have the guts to spend US$ 20 million? If you get there, I am prepared to invest up to US$ 200 million.' The second part took me by surprise and I just mumbled an answer.

What he was challenging me to do was to have the courage to put money where my mouth was. At the same time, he was making a statement of confidence in the initiative and in my incubating it. He implied 'enough of conceptualization, get on with execution.'

MANDATE

Mukesh Ambani instituted an experiment long before researchers at Reliance Life Sciences got their hands on shake-flasks and small-scale bioreactors. This was in the very creation of Reliance Life Sciences. 'You create your own support groups in Reliance Life Sciences and do not be weighed down by the Reliance system,' he told me. Having worked with him in several sectors, I knew he was apprehensive about bureaucracy creeping into Reliance and stifling innovation, and thought he was referring to that. But, in this case, what he meant to say was that Reliance Life Sciences would have to be a node for innovation, a node that was not weighed down by the bureaucracy of the large Reliance organization. At the same time, the large Reliance organization would need to give Reliance Life Sciences access to some of the strengths inherent in its support functions.

SEED QUALITY

As you sow, so shall you reap, goes the adage. This is very true for the start of a business. The less you know of the intricacies, science, technology and evolution of the business, the more time and effort you are compelled to put into conceptualizing, configuring and designing it. It pays to be agile and flexible. It pays even more to move gradually in the exposure of resources—human, material, financial and information. The quality of the seeding of the business will soon show up.

In other words, the newer you are to a business, the more you need to invest in understanding diverse perspectives and the dynamics of the business. If intensity is lacking in the quest, you could pay a big price when you are further and deeper into the business.

3

GETTING TRACTION WITH TALENT

'Capability of a business lies in the expanse of its peoples' minds.'

The greatest challenge for leadership is in seeding, nurturing and growing the organization. And, in the process, providing growth opportunities for people. People work for people first, then for the organization.

It is idealistic to look for talent that fully fits the bill. Look for people who may not be there cent per cent, but are game to bet on the opportunity and locate their own future within it. Stay away from folks with a baggage of know-all and inflated egos. Constantly realize the responsibility you have for people who came on board when you had nothing to show, but only a portrayal of the future.

Understand that human beings are complex and unpredictable. Every individual is different. Each one of them has the potential and power for development and transformation. This is not easy to fathom, but an imperative to harness in order to build and grow the organization.

We often underestimate the innate power in each one of us. Every one of us has a turbo in reserve that can be fired to get that extra burst of energy when the organization or family situation demands.

EARLY BIRDS

With the support of DHA and Mukesh Ambani, Reliance Life Sciences Private Limited was formed as an independent legal entity on 30 January 2001. In 2002, we went on to create a standalone organization around the development plan prepared by us. With the help of Sushil Khurana and Ravi Verma of the HR team in Reliance Industries, we hired a small leadership team for the new organization. Like me, both Sushil and Ravi had no clue about the biotechnology industry and the professionals who worked in it. Sushil had been a human resources development professional in the consumer goods industry and in the telecom industry. He was part of Reliance's infocomm venture and had gravitated to Reliance Life Sciences. Ravi also had an information technology human resources background.

Unfortunately, Sushil passed away due to a cardiac arrest so Ravi Verma and I had to scout for talent among the Indian scientific community and among Indians returning from overseas. We made several trips across India and a few to the US in search of talent. We would hold interviews from morning till late evening, and mostly did marketing pitches to deserving prospective candidates.

Among the earliest to join the new organization was Dr Venkata Ramana. He is credited with having developed the first low-cost recombinant hepatitis B vaccine in India, as part of Shantha Biotech, Hyderabad. A self-effacing scientist, Ramana was modesty personified. He knew that we had nothing to show and placed trust in my description of what we wanted to achieve and the promise of the larger vision. Today, he is our chief scientific officer and remains the self-effacing person that I had first met.

Ramana began to work in Maker Chambers, the head office of Reliance. We worked on plans to develop a wide range of biosimilars. I felt sorry for him—imagine a successful scientist, uprooted from Hyderabad with his family, working in a cubicle in an office in Mumbai. His boundless patience kept him going. Together, we decided to move ahead with building the laboratories first.

Another person to join early on, was Vivek Shinde. He was mandated to head administration. Soon enough, Vivek had to take care of procurement. He had no clue about what was to come, but stayed on anyway. He is a good organizer and manages the external interface, dealing with both the local law enforcers and the law breakers. Vivek comes to me only when something needs my intervention. Basil Gonsalves, who joined the administration team with Vivek, is quiet and works with a sense of purpose. He independently manages the administration of our first manufacturing plant for plasma proteins.

I cannot help but highlight the role of P.V. Raju, a former colleague from Indian Petrochemicals Corporation Limited, in the organization. He was employed in Mukesh Ambani's office and worked with me part-time, initially. However, Raju was soon spending most of his time with Reliance Life Sciences, and eventually transitioned to a full-time engagement. I encouraged him to do an MBA, which he did. I then gave him the mandate to lead human resources. I was frustrated with some human resource professionals who sounded great on concepts, but fell far below expectation on employee engagement, HR transactions and compliance. Much later in our evolution, I requested Raju to oversee materials and accounts cash flows, which he did admirably, in his inimitable style. Raju is extremely meticulous, anticipates what is required and takes action, instead of waiting to be told what to do. Once he makes a commitment, he always delivers.

SCIENCE ON PAPER

Dr Jacqueline Dias worked on conceiving the laboratory infrastructure, furniture, equipment and layout for Reliance

Life Sciences. Firdaus Pallonji, who joined us to maintain laboratory equipment and instruments, supported the effort. A very meticulous, fastidious person who takes a lot of pride in his work, Firdaus would move heaven and earth to get things done. To this day, Reliance Life Sciences banks on him to keep equipment in good condition. Firdaus, who is a devout Parsi, has given me some insights into Zoroastrianism.

Here we were, a molecular biologist, Ramana, working paper plans, another scientist, Jacqueline, designing laboratories, an electronics professional, Firdaus, sitting in judgement on buying laboratory equipment and maintaining it, Basil and Raju holding forth on administrative matters, Vivek managing internal and external interfaces—a motley mix of simple-minded folks who got a business up and running. All these individuals helped build the foundation of Reliance Life Sciences and today, are enjoying the fruits of their labour. They are fine examples of our hands-on style of management. In hindsight, science on paper led to clarity of thought. Many aspects of the scientific programmes, physical projects and business initiatives that we took up were first expressed in writing and then debated. Having a certain level of clarity, even if it was not perfect, helped minimize surprises during execution.

We did not leave it to serendipity to illuminate the science side of Reliance Life Sciences. We banked on young greenhorns, who though inexperienced were thoroughly competent professionals, for the planning and execution process.

EARLY DRIVERS OF DEVELOPMENT

Dr Sumit Misra, who had a background in Ranbaxy and Transasia Medical, joined us in 2001 to head marketing. He also had additional responsibility for regulatory affairs. A professional who had a strong sense of purpose, Sumit would travel all over the country, meeting doctors, hospitals and distributors and opening up business avenues. He had the ability to go after an opportunity and deal with the toughest of doctors and hospitals. Sumit also came up against non-believers among doctors and hospital staff, but won them over.

Sumit and I would often travel to meet doctors from varied disciplines. During a visit to Apollo Hospital, Delhi, part of a leading hospital chain in India, I did what had been unimaginable to me—I gave a lecture on life sciences to a group of doctors and paramedics. It was Sumit who had persuaded me to speak in this difficult and demanding setting. Much later, in 2007, Sumit joined Johnson & Johnson. However, in 2014, he returned to Reliance Life Sciences to head a new domain of development in advanced wound management products. He has been fulfilling this responsibility with flourish—straddling research, product development, manufacturing and market development.

Sumit had a chance meeting with Dr Chandra Viswanathan in 2002 and brought her skill sets to my attention. An MD and PhD., with expertise in hematology and transfusion medicine, Chandra had built a small commercial plasma fractionation centre as part of a large public hospital in Mumbai—King Edward Memorial Hospital, popularly known as KEM Hospital. Sumit and I went to meet Chandra in her office in KEM Hospital and I offered her the opportunity to be part of Reliance Life Sciences. She accepted willingly.

I distinctly remember the meeting she later had with Mukesh Ambani in Reliance Industries' new swanky office in the Fort area of Mumbai. She highlighted the similarities between petroleum refining and plasma fractionation. She explained that the market opportunity in India for plasma proteins was for one million litres of plasma fractionation per year while the KEM Hospital facility had a capacity of 10,000 litres. She was able to convince Mukesh Ambani, both about her abilities and about the opportunity in plasma proteins.

This was how Reliance Life Sciences invested in the plasma proteins business, which is a mainstream business for the company today. We continue to be the only end-to-end plasma to proteins manufacturer in South Asia, and are among a handful of players in the world. We established research and manufacturing in this domain and nurtured the initial team. Chandra moved on to head hematopoietic stem cells research and then the entire 'regenerative medicine' initiative. She continues to lead regenerative medicine, apart from working on developing a range of specialty plasma proteins.

It was at the KEM Hospital plasma fractionation centre that Sumit and I met Dr Manjunath Kamath. He later joined us as head of manufacturing for plasma proteins. Kamath is a quiet and deep individual, with a tremendous understanding of protein chemistry. He has been the prime mover in the setting up of the manufacturing facilities for plasma proteins. I have never seen Kamath getting restless, irritated or upset. As the adage goes, still waters run deep.

B. Srinivasan, whom I first met during my frequent visits to Goa and Jamnagar to support the agriculture initiative and the Jamnagar Greenbelt development project, later came to join our life sciences initiative. He had a corporate business development background and was part of the 40 MW independent gas-based power plant and agriculture initiatives led by Pascal Noronha in Goa. Srini has this insatiable thirst for information on industry and technology and helped me in understanding biotechnology and other technology domains. He supported the development of Reliance Life Sciences and continues to be involved in incubating a host of new initiatives for the Reliance group, operating out of the chairman's office.

Ravi Verma and I also motivated Dr Harinarayana Rao, one of the foremost animal research specialists in the country, to join us as head of animal research. Dr Rao used to head the animal research facility at the Centre for Cellular and Molecular Biology, Hyderabad. He walked away from the comfortable position that he had in his native environs of Hyderabad to join a new company that had nothing to talk about in animal research. Well respected, Dr Rao has had a very successful track record in obtaining regulatory approvals at Reliance Life Sciences.

Jamila Joseph is another resource who provided a fillip to development. She came from Quintiles India, which is part of Quintiles Transnational, the world leader in clinical research. Jamila has a quiet resolve and an in-depth knowledge and understanding of the clinical research industry in India—a rare combination of development focus and business development flair. For a short period of time, she was reporting to a hemato-oncologist whose aspirations lay beyond the confines of Reliance Life Sciences. He left the company abruptly, leaving Jamila to take charge of clinical research.

Jamila travelled alone to the US to get our first client, or 'sponsor' of clinical studies as they are known in the industry. Getting our first client so quickly was a pleasant surprise. I still remember working with Jamila in developing our first client presentation on clinical research. I used to join a few client business development meetings and we often had to wait endlessly at the offices of big pharmaceutical companies despite having confirmed appointments. These potential clients may have thought that we were new kids on the block who did not matter much, but this didn't deter us and we persisted.

Jamila continues to lead the clinical research business and is focusing on scaling up. She is one colleague who I regularly request to critically review my presentations and external communications. She invariably comes up with detailed corrections and comments. I rarely question her judgement in clinical research matters, and only provide guidance and support when it is required. Jamila, like many others in Reliance Life Sciences, enjoys the latitude that she has earned.

EARLY FUNCTIONAL LEADERS

Managers in support functions soon joined the early developers of Reliance Life Sciences, giving momentum to the leadership team. All these leaders continue with the company to this date, and have grown both in terms of their career and expanse of engagement.

Purnima Malkani joined us to lead the legal and intellectual property function. I have great admiration for her meticulous work, application of mind and independence of views. I make it a point to sign any legal document only if Purnima has reviewed it—and I make this known to all management team colleagues. In a lighter vein, I often joke that if Purnima sent me my resignation letter for my signature, I would sign it without batting an eyelid! Purnima has been forthright about her views on certain legal positions, and to her credit, would clarify what a legal call was and what a business call was, thereby setting clear boundaries for decision-making. A workaholic, she can be trusted to ensure proper diligence in legal aspects and litigations.

One day, Rahul Padhye, a civil engineer involved in infrastructure projects development, asked me if he could work in life sciences. He was completing a one-year business management programme at the Indian Institute of Management, Bengaluru (IIM-B). This programme was exclusively designed for Reliance engineers and was titled 'Management Programme for Reliance Engineers (MPRE)'. His request came when I had gone to IIM-B to present a guest lecture to MPRE participants, which I often used to do. Having watched him closely during my involvement in supporting infrastructure projects development, I had no hesitation in agreeing to his request.

On several occasions, Rahul would come to me in frustration and I would step in and facilitate matters. He led our biosimilars business, after an initial stint in the early days of the pharmaceutical business and is focused on scaling up. I call Rahul a 'sure-shot'. This is a term I use for team members who only have to be told half a sentence of instructions, and know exactly what is required and deliver. They only revert if they are stuck.

The other sure-shot in Reliance Life Sciences is S. Venkatesh, marketing head for the past few years. Venkatesh amazes me. He has this 'fire-in-the-belly' and a 'do-or-die attitude' and has an obsession for achieving targets. Venkatesh is demanding when it comes to the performance of his team members, and motivates them to deliver. I often stretch him on targets and he never fails me. Venkatesh has the rare ability to deal with the most difficult of doctors and hospital pharmacies only to emerge with wins that are mutually beneficial. Venkatesh is a person who does not tolerate attitude and integrity issues. He also does not take 'no' for an answer. He has built a small but strong marketing team of similar-minded professionals.

Santhosh Mathai, an electrical engineer by training and an MPRE product, who had worked in the Patalganga and Hazira petrochemical complexes of Reliance Industries and briefly for the infocomm initiative, expressed a desire to join Reliance Life Sciences. I agreed to his request without any hesitation. Today he heads the pharmaceutical business, which was reconfigured after an initial plan to be a large generic pharma company, following the global financial meltdown in 2008. Santhosh exemplifies maturity of thinking and leadership. He combines a calm approach with a strong focus on discipline and team work.

Another individual who exhibits personality and leadership traits similar to Santhosh, is Anand Vaze, who heads capital procurement. Always smiling and cool, Anand can be fully trusted with taking the right decisions with integrity.

An important resource person and an early development driver has been Dinesh Sathe. When I first met him and learnt that he was with Merck Sharp & Dhome (MSD), later known as Merind India, I immediately called up my twin brother who had worked there. He told me, 'Simply close your eyes and hire him.' So we did. Today, Dinesh is our chief operating officer. He has been responsible for not only building all our manufacturing facilities, but also creating a small team that can conceptualize, engineer and construct biopharmaceutical facilities. I often differ with him on some engineering matter and invariably one of us wins the point and the other concedes defeat graciously. He is a hands-on person and on top of every aspect and situation.

Sandip Mane works with Dinesh on engineering management and Manoj Dubey on construction management. They are two quiet, competent and tenacious professionals who never let issues bog them down or worry about my often unreasonable demands on stretched targets. They smile and invariably come up with a solution.

Gopal Rangaraj, a chemical engineer from NIT, Tiruchirapalli, who was part of the linear alkyl benzene manufacturing facility at the Patalganga site of Reliance Industries, had worked with me when I was in corporate business development in Maker Chambers. He left Reliance to work for SAP. I subsequently met Gopal in Bangalore and encouraged him to come back to Reliance, which he did as head of information technology. This was after Daniel Sequeira, who joined Reliance Life Sciences in 2001, chose to leave and be part of the larger information technology team at Reliance Industries Limited. A quiet and competent individual, Danny incubated and led the information technology group, rolled out software and set up infrastructure and systems.

Dr Arnab Kapat is a doctorate in biochemical engineering and biotechnology from the Indian Institute of Technology, Madras and was involved with process development for therapeutic proteins in the early years. He responded enthusiastically to the imperative of creating a competency development institute within Reliance Life Sciences. We call it Reliance Institute of Life Sciences (RILS), a not-for-profit organization focused on competency development tailored to the biopharmaceutical domain and steering external education-driven academic partnerships. Hundreds of entry-level students and professionals enrolled in courses of RILS as well as RLS employees pursuing masters and doctoral programmes, have had their academic pursuits shaped by Arnab.

With Arnab leading competency development and my decision to get back to nurture and support talent, low profile Raju was left to focus on employee engagement, and transactional, compliance and audit issues. Raju is ably assisted by Pramod Shanbhag, head of revenue procurement and Surendra Deodhar, head of materials management. Both of them are veterans in the company with high levels of integrity. They often had to patiently deal with irate vendors facing payment issues during periods of working capital squeeze, in the scaling-up years. They balance the demands for materials from internal users, with my own demands for working capital productivity, material productivity and relentless cost reduction opportunities.

Later in our evolution, Ravishankar Kasturi joined as head of process development for biopharmaceuticals. After a good track record, he took additional responsibility for manufacturing. Here he brought into play his intimate knowledge and feel for the processes. This ability, combined with his hands-on approach, saw dramatic results in product yield improvements, while maintaining consistently high quality. Ravi has a calm and quiet demeanour. His character reminds you of the adage 'still waters run deep'.

LIVING IN PAST GLORY

Being inexperienced, we erred in the initial team composition—we hired senior team leaders who were in their early fifties. At the same time, we also hired relatively younger people. The experience levels were mixed. Most of the senior members of the team came with loads of baggage which soon manifested in their work.

'When I was in ABC organization, we used to do things like this,' or 'When I was in XYZ organization this is how we were organized,' were oft-repeated dialogues. Internally, they could not reconcile to their present organization and help shape its future. Those of us who were ingrained in the Reliance way of working, where past accomplishments were history and what mattered was 'current value', were amused. But, out of courtesy, we did not confront these senior leaders.

INDIVIDUAL AGGRANDIZEMENT

Other organizational issues revolved around those scientists who came from purely academic research organizations or those who were practising medical professionals. The 'I' factor was very strong. They asked questions such as:

'How can a science-based organization be led by a non-science person?'

'How can a purchase group take buying decisions?'

'Why can't I be given a certain budget or grant and be free to buy what I want or hire whom I want?'

'Who are you to question the work I do?'

'Why should we have weekly review meetings?'

'Why can't I collaborate with an institution or scientist of my choice?'

All these questions led us to believe that many scientists and practising medical professionals saw themselves as above the organization. This was very unlike those who came from private research laboratories and medical professionals who had built institutions, big or small, or those who had faced failures in their past engagements. Such egocentric and self-centred individuals created barriers for collaboration. They had their own views about how research should be managed. They had their own favourites in so far as scientific collaborators and vendors for supply of equipment or consumables were concerned. One of them insisted that oxygen supply must be from a particular vendor. Others questioned why purchase decisions must be made by procurement. The Reliance ethos mandated that technical decisions and procurement decisions must be delineated, and decisions were open to reviews, compliances and audits.

Vinay Ranade, who joined us early on, was responsible for finance and commercial matters. He was a chartered accountant and had done his MBA from the Asian Institute of Management, Manila. A fine professional with high integrity, Vinay is always willing to take on unchartered or unfamiliar responsibilities. Today, he heads the plasma proteins business. He doubles up as CEO of Reliance GeneMedix, a subsidiary of Reliance Life Sciences. Reliance GeneMedix was acquired in December 2006.

As head of procurement, Vinay was often bullied on purchasing decisions by the strong-headed and egoistic scientists. I did not approve of this and had to put my foot down to uphold his role and decision-making authority. I also had to insulate Vinay from one particular individual in the Reliance system who wanted an order to go to a particular vendor.

One of the best things in Reliance is that, once there is confidence in a leader's decision-making abilities, system and process conformance, the leader is given full freedom to decide. But, I must stress that this confidence has to be earned and is not an entitlement linked to positions or titles.

In essence, we would not tolerate the tantrums of the egoistic leaders and held our ground. As it happened, all these individuals had a graceful exit, encouraged by Reliance.

SHORTCOMINGS

All the team members who joined early on, were not the epitome of excellence in their discipline or managerial competence. As with all human beings, including myself, they had their shortcomings. The pace they wanted to work at did not always match my demands. Sometimes they would baulk at stretched targets. My shortcomings were impatience, occasionally being too demanding and, at times, openly expressing my frustrations. I had to spend quite some time smoothening the sharp edges of team members, honing their soft skills, understanding their personal issues and offering solutions and support.

I could not tolerate doing experiments and engaging with projects endlessly without achieving tangible outcomes in a reasonable time. In my opinion, science has a definitive purpose. Every scientist should know when a dead end has been reached and have the courage to say so.

I believed it was important for Reliance Life Sciences to drop science projects which were not making progress. This created heartburn, no doubt. But Reliance has been ruthless on this aspect. Otherwise, some projects would have received funding based on their glamour and fad value while other deserving projects would have suffered.

POWER OF COMMITMENT

All the individuals who joined Reliance Life Sciences in its budding years exuded passion. Almost all of them were young, in their thirties, when I encouraged them to come on board. Since they were largely greenhorns, they saw their future in the future of Reliance Life Sciences. In contrast, the so-called industry experts came with enormous egos. They sought self glory in the media and were a deterrent to development.

There were many others who came on board as passengers. They believed that they were on a train to nowhere, made pronouncements to this effect and then left for greener pastures. Periodically, I bump into some of these people. Realizing that Reliance Life Sciences has survived, and looking for a safe harbour in their troubled times, they express a desire to come back. I don't mind re-hiring individuals who had a good track record with us, but I refuse to consider those who did not.

All the employees who joined Reliance Life Sciences in the early years and have stayed on, placed their trust in the company, in me and in our collective future. In turn, they placed a huge responsibility on me—not to let them down. As a result, I remained loyal to Reliance Life Sciences and never considered job opportunities outside the company.

All the young leaders have been with Reliance Life Sciences for a long time and have contributed to building the foundation. They didn't run away when they were frustrated, they didn't walk away from challenges, and they didn't believe in naysayers. On the contrary, they were passionate, stayed focused and believed in themselves and the organization. None of them declined my requests, whether this was to work outside India, move to a new domain, or to close down a project or facility that was not doing well. The power of youth, passion and engagement continues to amaze me.

Often I ask myself, what is next for them. I have never asked myself, 'What is next for me?'

4

STARTING SMALL...SOMEWHERE

'It is important to fail small and early.'

New businesses that require an infrastructure, in the form of an office, a research laboratory, a manufacturing facility or a services centre, cannot be fixated on getting all that is required in the manner envisaged and in a place of choice. Such a business could be stillborn. It is important to swallow one's pride, start small, start somewhere and get into the flow. Resources are enhanced with advancement and evolution.

DON'T ASK FOR THE MOON

Getting access to space in Reliance is always a challenge, more so in Mumbai where the cost of real estate is among the highest in the world. In the early days at Reliance Life Sciences, space was not only in short supply, but had many takers.

Being new kids on the block, we had to present a convincing argument for space, to avoid losing out to the more robust and muscular businesses within Reliance. We had to learn to not ask for the moon but be content with those spaces that other companies in the group did not want.

BENCH SPACE

In 1997, Reliance took over the management of HN Hospital in south Mumbai with the intention of transforming it into a state-of-the-art tertiary care hospital. The trust that managed HN Hospital had no funds. Reliance had committed to equipping it and managing it to provide patients with modern medical care.

I did the unthinkable at that time. I requested for a couple of floors in an unused shell of the hospital building, on the condition that it would be surrendered later. Since I asked for space that did not matter to others, it was granted without much ado. Thus, the first laboratory infrastructure was created. I realized that instead of making big demands, it was better to ask for small resources since there was a higher probability of getting these approved.

Work started on medical biotechnology in the laboratories at HN Hospital. As a molecular biologist, Jacqueline Dias would walk the length and breadth of the two floors of the HN Hospital building, flourishing a measuring tape to gauge and design spaces to the last detail. The laboratories were very functional and looked good as well. We had laboratories for embryonic stem cells, hematopoietic stem cells, skin and tissue engineering, molecular medicine, recombinant proteins, plasma proteins, small-molecule drug discovery, plant metabolic engineering, assisted reproduction and a stem cell-enriched cord blood repository.

BEING REFUGEES

In a similar vein, we were looking at lab space for the plant tissue culture and industrial biotechnology facilities. We asked for and were given an unused site support office (SSO) area in the Jamnagar refinery and petrochemicals complex project construction offices area. These were temporary tin-sheet roof office buildings made during the construction phase of the

Jamnagar project. The SSO building that we got was way past its utility. The surrounding area was dusty, given that it was a construction site, the largest in India. We could not complain and had to be content with any space that we could lay our hands on. A tiny plot of land was available outside the refinery complex, and we built a very small aloe vera processing facility there.

When it came to office space, the propensity to be displaced was higher and we did get dislodged by other initiatives in the Reliance group perceived to have higher priority. We were first allotted space in Maker Chambers in south Mumbai, near the locus of power, and later we shifted to the Shriram Mills complex in central Mumbai.

One day, Mukesh Ambani told me candidly that life sciences was an 'overhead'. He suggested that we move our offices to the Sewri area in south east Mumbai. It did hurt to be called an overhead, but that was the truth. Our resolve to be profitable, therefore, became even stronger. Sewri, part of the underbelly of Mumbai, housed the large warehouse of an erstwhile polyester company, Terene Fibres India Limited of ICI, UK, that Reliance had acquired and converted into an office space. We had no choice but to move there.

The daily commute to the Sewri office was pretty depressing and required tenacity and endurance. You had to drive on poor quality roads past squalor and the long stretch of warehouses belonging to the Food Corporation of India and the deserted Mumbai docks. The area appeared eerie and deserted late in the evening. However, once you reached the office, you felt you were in an oasis!

The work we were doing in plasma proteins soon required that we build a pilot-scale manufacturing facility not far from the laboratories in HN hospital. We opted for an old textile factory building in central Mumbai that had been recently acquired by the Reliance group. It was a strange place for a manufacturing facility but what mattered to us was the robust building shell. We pitched for the space and were granted it.

Rahul Padhye was mandated to develop this building into a small plasma protein manufacturing facility. He willingly accepted, probably not knowing what he was walking into. He liked my idea of starting modestly and investing in manufacturing if we wanted to get scale. Despite facing several obstacles, including local regulatory problems and vendor and contractor issues, Rahul did a creditable job by completing the facility in just three months. Thus, we entered manufacturing at Reliance Life Sciences.

A HOME AT LAST

Reliance Life Sciences started out as a migrant within the Reliance group, with its facilities scattered across different locations. We longed for a place to call 'home' and felt very much like those people who live in leased properties and look forward to having a home of their own. We also had to live with the label of being the underdogs of the group and show the rest that we were capable and were not dependent on others' mercies. In a large conglomerate rooted in traditional commodity businesses, patience tends to be low.

Things started to change when Reliance Industries acquired IPCL, my former company, in the year 2002. Two years later, in 2004, it was decided to move the catalyst manufacturing facility of the erstwhile IPCL out of its 20-acre campus in Navi Mumbai. We had a potential place for our campus since there were no other takers for this modest property. We could not have asked for more. We pitched for it. Mukesh Ambani agreed. The main issue in making the piece of land available to us was dealing with the unionized employees of IPCL on that site. The negotiations were protracted.

In the meantime, we got Venkataramanan Associates of Bangalore, which was associated with some other Reliance sites, to develop the master plan. This plan duly went through the review and approval processes but remained on paper until the site became available to us.

Eventually, I requested Mukesh Ambani to intervene in the union matter. He spoke to V.V. Bhat, a long-time head of human resources in the group, and sought a quick closure. The settlement came through. We took up the task of building a new campus after breaking down the old and dilapidated structures. Reliance Life Sciences would have a home at last. We named the life sciences complex the 'Dhirubhai Ambani Life Sciences Centre' in honour of DHA. Now, the challenge was to build the campus and make it profitable.

TRYST WITH DESTINY

Hindu philosophy believes in the inevitability of destiny or fate. 'You are destined to be what is ordained by God,' goes the saying. Many Hindus believe your fate is written on your forehead before you are born. Even if a person is poor, he or she believes that it is in their fate to be poor, rarely questioning why it should be that way. 'Whatever has to happen will happen,' and 'Whatever can go wrong, will go wrong' are common beliefs.

Belief in destiny was alien to me. My father had always told me and my three siblings to eschew superstition. 'Accept only what is proved by science,' he would say. At times, he would explain the scientific rationale behind some religious practices, including those with roots in psychology. He would look for scientific meaning in the practices and discard them if they did not make scientific sense. My father would say that we reap the benefits of our labour, and any wealth not earned from honest hard work would not stay with us.

In contrast, my mother was superstitious and hated to be in situations which she considered inauspicious. For instance, it is considered inauspicious to see buffaloes when setting out on a journey; it doesn't matter if the journey is short or long. In the early seventies, there were buffaloes galore roaming the roads of Bangalore, where we lived at that time. Housewives in the city preferred to get fresh milk from cows and buffaloes delivered to their doorstep, therefore, milkmen would go from house to house with cows and buffaloes to deliver the fresh milk. My father didn't believe in this superstition and didn't hesitate to set out in our car on a road with buffaloes. When my mother protested, he would advise her to keep her head down and not look up.

While my father rejected superstitions and individuals who called themselves god men, he was a spiritual person and saw religion as a way of life and an avenue to find inner peace. Though I did not relate to superstition and god men, the life sciences campus was like a tryst with destiny for me. It was either a very rare coincidence or an example of compound probability in practice, depending on how you looked at it.

Here is how my tryst with the life sciences campus occurred: When I graduated from IIM, Ahmedabad, I had a techno-commercial job offer from Associated Cement Companies (ACC). It was for their catalyst and adsorbents division, called CATAD. In 1980, during my summer internship at British Paints (now known as Berger Paints), Mumbai branch, I was doing a survey on anti-corrosive paints and travelled the length and breadth of Mumbai's industrial locales. It was during this time that I visited the ACC CATAD site a couple of times. It was a loss-making division engaged in the manufacture of low-value activated alumina, adsorbents and molecular sieves.

IPCL had been searching for a site to manufacture the specialty catalysts that its research and development centre had developed, and acquired this CATAD division from ACC in 1987. IPCL transformed the CATAD division's product mix and made it profitable. It was a very rare case of a public sector company buying a loss-making private sector unit and turning it profitable. Here was another example of creative destruction.

In April 1994, I left IPCL to join Reliance, where in 2005, I was again associated with the same site. I had a mandate to transform it once again, this time from a catalyst and adsorbents manufacturing facility to a life sciences complex. This was the third time I was associated with the campus site—the first time my association was brief, the second time it was more frequent and the third time I was actually operating out of this campus.

5

ANCHORING THE FOUNDATION

'Factoring for fuzziness prepares frontier
businesses for imponderables.'

*Waiting for a facility to be fully done before moving in could
be futile. It is better to move in and make things happen.
Apart from giving a sense of ownership and responsibility,
it reduces cash burn and gets programmes into higher gear.*

*It is rarely that there is an upfront vision of what the
eventual initiative would look like in its engagements, scale,
flows and character. As the business unfolds, there can be
several unforeseen resource demands. Therefore, it makes sense
to provide for grey boxes, in the form of land, space or options,
in the early stage of planning. An element of fuzziness helps
in factoring future needs.*

CONCEPTUAL OBSCURITY

The task of planning, designing and developing a life sciences
campus site was daunting. How would we house biotechnology
facilities in twenty acres of land, I wondered, when I was still
getting acquainted with this industry. It was clear to us that we
needed an integrated campus that included everything from

laboratory research, pre-clinical research, clinical development, and manufacturing to marketing. The campus also had to be diverse, encompassing several areas in biotechnology. It was also evident that to balance risks and rewards, we had to provide a place for the services business.

Some of us decided to start with conceptualizing the campus. Fortunately we did not have to deal with the egoistic leaders who came on board in the initial years of Reliance Life Sciences, and left soon after. Neither were we anchored in the past in our thought processes. Being tentative, we played safe.

While providing for laboratory research facilities, we decided to keep some extra space that may be required to accommodate any additional facilities, if and when we grew. We kept a couple of floors open for custom research for clients with independent access control. My knowledge of civil engineering, project management and corporate development, helped me with space planning. My engagement with the Jamnagar site of Reliance Industries had also equipped me with the confidence to take on a larger piece of canvas and get creative with it.

KIDS WITH LEGO BLOCKS

While developing the life sciences campus, we were like kids with colourful Lego blocks. We were neither scared nor overwhelmed. Being in either state would have hindered our ability to get the site completed in time. We did not know the shape of things to come, but kept going anyway.

Today, there is a vast difference between the ideas we had started out with and what we finally achieved. The additional but unused spaces give us the ability to spend on capital projects and grow facilities commensurate with growth in the business. Having such unused spaces would make traditional, rigid-minded investors scorn. But within the Reliance system, where constant growth is ingrained in the DNA of the organization, elbow room for growth, physically and figuratively, is a necessity.

JAMNAGAR INSPIRATION

A number of Reliance Industries' professionals supported us while the life sciences campus was being constructed between the years 2003 and 2005. A few individuals stand out, e.g. A.G. Dawda, a veteran construction professional, who had left his senior position in a Middle East company to join Reliance Industries as the head of construction of the Jamnagar petroleum refinery. This was no mean job. The Jamnagar site, at that time, was a massive 10,000 acres and became the largest petroleum refining site in the world. This is ironic given that India imports about 80 per cent of its energy needs. Today, the site is spread over 20,000 acres and encompasses two world-scale refineries, petrochemical plants, a petroleum coke gasification plant and several power generation facilities. In addition, it is home to a port, a jetty and a large marine tankage facility for product imports and exports.

My association with Jamnagar goes back to its pre-development phase. An exceptionally talented, US-trained, former colleague, Pascal Noronha and I assembled a competent team that was instrumental in developing green belts, horticulture plantations, agro-forestry and landscaping. The team also developed mangroves to support the coastal ecology. We derived great satisfaction in developing about 2,000 acres of semi-arid, dusty and dry land into a rich and visually-appealing, green environment. Today, Jamnagar is home to the largest mango orchard in the country. The green area has become a must-see spot for company guests visiting Jamnagar.

Every time I visited Jamnagar, I felt in awe of its sheer expanse, just the way one would feel gazing at the stars and the unknown universe beyond, on a clear starry night. Jamnagar taught me the value of meticulous execution. It also taught me to take very imposing problems bit by bit and resolve them, without missing the larger objectives at hand. Compared to Reliance's Jamnagar site, the life sciences site was puny. But for us, it was home and the complexity mattered more than the size.

GRAMS VS KILOGRAMS

The Jamnagar complex was on a very different scale compared to the Reliance Life Sciences campus. Regarding dimensions, if the larger Reliance Industries talked about metric tons, we talked about grams, milligrams and micrograms, which are one millionth to a billionth in scale. If the larger Reliance Industries dealt with millions and billions of dollars, we dealt with millions of rupees.

In manufacturing operations, if the larger Reliance Industries talked about high temperature and high pressure reactors and processes, we talked about ambient temperatures and pressure bioreactors and processes. If the larger Reliance Industries talked about continuous processes, we talked about batch processes.

In decision-making, if the larger Reliance Industries talked about buying equipment such as gas turbines for captive power plants as if they were buying onions and potatoes, we talked about buying equipment as though we were buying precious metal.

We were in a microscopic world—the world of biotechnology, bioreactors, chromatography, microfiltration, nanofiltration, centrifuges and cold storage—which was in sharp contrast to the world of chemical technology, process reactors, large compressors and distillation columns of our parent company. We were dealing with life, living and living systems, while they were dealing with synthesis and synthetics. In short, we were in a world that was vastly different from our parentage.

DIFFERENT BUT SIMILAR

In largely mono-cultural environments, it is tough to be different. We were in such a context. The larger Reliance Industries, till it got into organized retail, and information and communication businesses, was, by and large, mono-cultural. Some people tended to see systems, policies and processes in a one-size-fits-all manner. This had its internal challenges with the policies, systems, processes and attitudes of the larger environment imposed on us. At times we would protest, especially with the service levels of the central shared services group. The concept of central shared services in a large conglomerate is excellent. However, in the absence of sensitivity and flexibility to the specific demands of the individual businesses that constitute a conglomerate, it becomes restrictive.

On the other hand, there were similarities with the larger Reliance Industries. This was certainly true in the expanse of our thinking and the accent on conforming to systems, processes, project conceptualization and execution. For us, Reliance Industries was like an elder and successful sibling; an organization that inspired and could be emulated. At Reliance Life Sciences, we seek to imbibe much of the larger Reliance's consensus-based corporate business development, expansive formats of thinking, detailed planning, meticulous execution, financial management prowess, operational efficiencies and project execution skills.

But some not so well-informed individuals within the organization and outside it, would compare us with the larger Reliance. They expected us to become a billion dollar company within a short time. This is akin to a child growing in the shadows of an extremely successful and famous parent. Sometimes this leads to opportunities for those with dynastic ambitions. We did not want to go down that path. We had to grow on our own strength and mettle. This was our resolve.

Albert Einstein's 'theory of relativity' applies to all walks of life. Everything is relative as the context expands in scope. As a company, we had our position in the relativity spectrum—a small dot in the Reliance group, and though we were big within the biotechnology space in India, we were still a dot in the global industry context.

Comparisons can be used to set goals and motivate participants. Comparisons should not be used to create expectations and stress. It is fine to benchmark, say, with best-in-class on performance metrics. But, not in superimposing or transplanting the same benchmark within a different context. Extreme performance is a product of years and years of hard work, dedication, focus and continuous improvement, powered by motivation. Reliance Industries tends to be spoken about for its size, scale and reach. Most often, this comes without an appreciation of the efforts of hundreds of thousands of committed teams and the leadership that has enabled it.

In India, there is a tendency to compare and make judgements such as 'there can be no problem for him/her, he/she has everything going for him/her'. I strongly discourage my colleagues from making such comments. I remind them of the saying, 'Only the wearer of the shoe knows where it pinches.' I told my wife soon after our marriage that if you compare yourself with others you will have sleepless nights. You must invest in yourself and grow. Compare only to be inspired and motivated and not to see how you fare in relation to the other person. This simple but profound philosophy governed our blooming years and will continue to do so, hopefully, forever.

MOVE IN TO MAKE THINGS HAPPEN

As the life sciences campus was nearing completion, I decided to move in there. I told Vivek Shinde and my colleagues, 'Let's not wait for everything to be ready. It will never happen unless we live and breathe the place.' This was based on my experience, since childhood, of periodically moving from one city to another city, given the transferable job that my father had. He would move first and then get things fixed. I used the same principle when I bought an apartment in Mumbai in 2004. It was not fully ready, but we moved in, engaged with the big and small issues and got them fixed.

When we moved into the life sciences campus in 2005, only the offices were close to readiness. We worked in the midst of dust, grime, noise and vibration from construction equipment and activities. But we were able to pitch our tents and make things happen. Otherwise, we would have waited for ever. We could take decisions on the spot. And, catch service providers on site to give them a daily set of 'punch points' to complete.

I once read a quote by Jim Lovell, which truly inspired me. According to it, there are three kinds of people:

Those who make things happen.
Those who watch things happen.
And, those who wonder what happened.

Good and aspiring leaders belong in the first category, not in the second and, least of all in the third category.

ELEPHANT IN THE ROOM

One big challenge that we faced in shifting from HN Hospital to the new life sciences campus was the movement of the cord blood stem cell repository. The large stainless steel tank that stored cord blood stem cells under liquid nitrogen was a 'delicate darling'. It could not tilt more than five degrees because the cells, which were in canisters suspended in a rack system within a liquid nitrogen pool maintained at -196°C, could dislodge and fall inside the tank. The liquid nitrogen had to be maintained at this temperature, otherwise the cells would die. The tank could not withstand nasty bumps on the road for the same reasons and had to be moved at a snail's pace. There could be major safety issues in case of liquid nitrogen spillage. We had to move it anyway. We were told that transport of such nature had not been done before. At stake were thousands of cord blood stem cell units that could be used in the future for saving patients' lives.

What followed was a meticulously planned and executed effort by a multi-disciplinary team. Every part of the route was mapped in great detail. This included movement on wooden supports from the HN Hospital building to the road, figuring out every gradient on every segment of the road, speed breakers and getting around Mumbai's famous and notorious potholes. Some of them could beat volcanic craters! Even traversing the last stretch from the road to the facility was a huge challenge.

The solution lay in designing and fabricating a strong load-bearing steel frame from which the tank could be suspended. This incorporated monitoring its level with reference to the ground, as well as the level of liquid nitrogen in order to alert roadside refilling, if required. The local traffic police was informed well in advance and, thankfully, provided support. Traffic on the route was studied. Movement at night was planned, mainly to minimize accidents en route, expected to be caused more by other vehicles than ours. In India, 95 per cent of road safety issues emanate from other drivers on the road! Finally, when it ended well, there was more relief than a sense of achievement.

FILLIP

The new campus gave Reliance Life Sciences a big fillip. Here was a world-class facility that we were proud of. At HN Hospital, we were apologetic with visitors and regulators. At the new facility, we welcomed visitors and showed them around with pride.

The manufacturing facilities for biosimilars and plasma proteins came up soon after we moved into the new campus. This helped us to scale up commercially. The laboratory animal research facility, amongst the best in Asia, with a clean room Class A 100* facility for studies on immune-compromised animals, helped get traction on our clinical development efforts. Every part of the campus had a role to play in the scaling up of Reliance Life Sciences.

Above all, the new campus infused confidence in employees and effectively neutralized the naysayers and critics. Investment in a 20-acre life sciences campus was evidence that Reliance Life Sciences was for real. However, moving from the confines and constraints of the laboratories in HN Hospital to our own campus created its own set of problems and challenges. All of a sudden, many scientists wanted more space and were in a 'space grab' mindset. We would have none of this, and reserved a good portion of the space for future expansion.

EXPAT'S CHALLENGE

One of the biggest issues and challenges that we faced was with the mechanical completion, validation and startup of the biopharmaceutical manufacturing facility. It housed the largest mammalian cell culture facility in India and continues to enjoy this status to this day. Unfortunately for Reliance Life Sciences, Aker Kvaerner, USA, the design and engineering services firm involved with the biopharmaceuticals manufacturing facility, decided midway through the project, that it would close down engagements with the pharmaceutical sector. Our project was passed on to the Indian arm of Aker Kvaerner. So, we had a serious problem on our hands. The biotechnology domain expertise in Aker Kvaerner, India was very limited. They focused mainly on the hydrocarbons sector. But we did not have the option of changing horses midway.

---

*A Class 100 clean room, as per international standards, means that not more than 100 particles of more than 0.5 microns are permitted per cubic feet of air, with no microbiological contamination in settling plates.

Around this time, we brought on board two expatriates, Mathew Bishop from the UK and Timothy Roy from the US. Tim had worked for Amgen, the largest biotech company at that time, and was involved in projects there. Tim was an aggressive project execution person by nature. Enormously talented, he did not like leaving a lot of things on the ground. Before hiring Mathew and Tim, we had engaged a small consulting firm in the US to review the design of Aker Kvaerner, USA from the viewpoint of conformance to USFDA standards; their suggestions were incorporated in the project.

I instituted a weekly review meeting at the highest level with officials of Aker Kvaerner, India, who were keen to see the end of our project, which was a distraction for them. To Aker Kvaerner's credit, Rama Iyer, managing director and Pothen Phillip, project director, participated in the Monday meetings in their office. Dinesh Sathe, who had joined us earlier as projects and engineering head, along with Tim, Mathew and myself would represent Reliance Life Sciences at these meetings.

One day, Tim barged into my room and claimed that, in his view, this project would take another three years to be completed. I told him that we could make every effort and get it done in one year. But he said he had given up and wanted to leave. I persuaded him to stay, but he was adamant and left Reliance Life Sciences soon after.

Having been challenged by Tim, my resolve became stronger to see the project through to execution. Along with Dinesh Sathe and Mathew Bishop, we got the project back on track and completed in one year. We stood vindicated! But Tim had sensitized us to two very important lessons: The first lesson was that it is important for any construction site to be treated like a 'clean room'. Unfortunately, this is not the case with projects in India and most construction sites are unclean and messy. We continue to struggle with contractors on sites to keep the construction workplace clean and tidy.

The second lesson was on safety during construction.

Fortunately, the Reliance group has had a strong safety culture and looked up to DuPont as a role model. So, early on, we hired Birendra Thakur, whose primary job was to ensure safety in construction. Birendra did a creditable job and continues to work with the same zeal. Later on, we worked towards getting the highest of global safety accreditations and maintaining them. But, safety is one aspect where you can never rest on your laurels. Even the best of companies have had an accident or two, despite a well-ingrained safety culture.

PERIODIC BUY-IN

A German expatriate Dr Rainer Pabst, who has been with us as head of plasma proteins manufacturing, told me of his experience in two transnational companies that he had worked for, one in Germany and the other in the US. He explained that a group would work on a plan and its implementation in detail and then the plan would be presented to the board of directors. If the plan and budgets were approved, the team focused on implementation.

In contrast, at Reliance Life Sciences, we would have a dynamic plan, which was a euphemism for lack of clarity. Rainer was initially uncomfortable to see the constant change in the demands of a programme or project team during execution. Later, he got used to it. In the corporate business development function, more so in Reliance, you have to learn to be comfortable working in an unstructured environment.

Reliance and Reliance Life Sciences rigorously value-engineer a project to get higher capital productivity. This enables them to have a competitive advantage throughout the economic life of the asset, more so for capital-intensive businesses. A weekly review of execution performance against the plan is made. This covers the physical progress and an assessment of the financial performance of the project. This is done at Mukesh Ambani's level, when any major project expenditure has to be made. Towards the later stage of a project, daily review meetings take place, again at the top management level.

Rainer now realizes that it makes sense for all programme and project team members to catch problems as they happen and resolve them in good time. It is better to do it this way, instead of doing a post-mortem in review meetings. Therefore, at Reliance Industries, an approved plan is a beginning. Reliance Life Sciences has gone through such a process for almost all its projects.

GROUND LESSONS

Getting the life sciences campus completed and bringing it to life taught us several important lessons. The first was that it is important to be on the ground to get a project completed.

The second lesson was to assess the situation, intensify engagement and work through a recovery plan, so that you don't get overwhelmed by setbacks. This is easier said than done as it requires resolve, clear thinking and a 'we can win' mindset.

The third was to factor in space to grow in the foreseeable future. This imposes a capital penalty, but pays far more in the medium term. Returns are in terms of saved time and costs, and most of all, in terms of the ability to conceptualize and provide for growth with fewer limitations when the opportunity is right.

The fourth was to constantly value-engineer a project to ensure its long-term competitive advantage.

6

GAINING MOMENTUM

'Breakthrough businesses breach
barricades in becoming.'

*As a new business gets going and growing, it moves from
one milestone to another. There are times when it moves
from one trajectory to another—entering new markets,
taking up new product groups for development, adding new
functional dimensions and initiating new organizational
transformations. A new altitude beckons when a lower one
is reached. Unanticipated setbacks should not unnerve, but
rather serve as rallying points for resolve and resurgence.*

*When gaining visibility, the responsibility on leadership
increases in new ways. Visibility is a double-edged sword.
With measured exposure, visibility is helpful. But, unrestrained
visibility, especially by leadership team members trying to bask
in the limelight, can be dysfunctional.*

*On another plane, visibility brings with it detractors, in
the form of the dark side of product-market competition and
targeted hiring of talent by competition. There are other factors,
such as encountering fair-weather friends, and greater scrutiny
by regulatory agencies, media and social activists. Navigating
through these situations calls for maturity in striking a balance
between seeking fulfilment and handling frustrations.*

On the positive side, visibility when manifested as tangible user benefits and goodwill, can be a great motivator for team members to perform and attain higher scales of achievement.

VISIBILITY

Reliance Life Sciences was getting to be known. We had a sense of not having arrived, but being somewhere on the road. In a long journey, there is no arrival, just short periods of rest before hitting the trail again. Awareness among constituencies brings visibility, some of it good and some not so good. Along with visibility come challenges. Since our inception, we worked with a mindset of being a low-profile outfit and letting our work speak for itself. This worked well for us. We wanted to continue that way. We were the least interested in shouting from the rooftops about our achievements.

Many companies were compelled to give out news every quarter, probably because they were listed on stock markets driven by positive quarterly sound bites. Other companies would rush press releases as soon as they received an approval from the Review Committee on Genetic Manipulation (RCGM) of the central Ministry of Science and Technology. They would do this with a great sense of accomplishment.

We found this strange since an approval from RCGM is just one step in the long and arduous process of getting regulatory approvals. Reliance Life Sciences has a deep product and clinical development pipeline of recombinant biosimilars and biosimilar monoclonal antibodies and we regularly attend RCGM meetings. Following the industry trend, we could have had frequent media releases. But we chose not to.

The people who mattered to us at Reliance Life Sciences recognized our work. These were doctors, hospitals, patient groups, policy planners, potential employees, competitors, some media professionals, academics, vendors and regulators. This was all that mattered to us.

UNRAVELLING

In August 2001, in the early days of Reliance Life Sciences, there was considerable media interest in us. We probably did not deserve all that media attention. The media interest increased after the National Institutes of Health (NIH) in the US, listed Reliance Life Sciences among the ten companies in the world working on embryonic stem cells. If embryonic cell lines were sourced by researchers in the US, the researchers would be eligible for government grants only if they sourced from one of the listed ten companies. While not much came out of this listing for Reliance Life Sciences in terms of business, it gave us significant visibility at a very early stage.

Along with this visibility came an internal challenge—self-aggrandizement by a senior manager. This was clearly the downside of visibility. One of the leaders responsible for a research programme misused the external recognition for personal aggrandizement. Interviews were given to the media without conforming to established organizational regulations. Often, the interviews would be done at home, as if to convey the message that the person in question was solely responsible for the recognition that Reliance Life Sciences was receiving.

I naturally raised an objection. Here was a case of serious non-compliance with company policies and corporate norms. This sort of personal aggrandizement was not in Reliance's interest. The response to the objection I raised was very vicious and vitriolic. I stood my ground. Matters escalated to Mukesh Ambani. In the meantime, other leaders, particularly in research, claimed that a non-scientist should not head a life sciences organization. This was clearly a reference to me.

Mukesh Ambani soon enough asked me what he should do about the matter. I told him, 'I leave the decision to your judgement and will go by what you decide.' When the problem persisted, I candidly told him, 'It will help if you can decide as to who should lead Reliance Life Sciences. If it's me, you know that I would be committed two hundred percent. Otherwise, I am happy to step back and work on another opportunity.' He responded, 'Fine.' I left it at that.

Mukesh Ambani asked a senior colleague in the Reliance group to meet a cross-section of leaders in Reliance Life Sciences. I presumed that the objective was to validate my leadership. I had no issue with this. As a leader, I had to be open to independent external validation of my leadership. I had to be willing to take constructive feedback and change myself if required.

Soon enough, the individual who had stirred up all the trouble had a facilitated disengagement from Reliance Life Sciences. Mukesh Ambani never discussed the matter with me and I never asked him about it. But, his implicit trust in me was evident. Peace returned for me. At a crucial time, I had to stand my ground in not tolerating someone hijacking the organization's standing for personal gain, even if it meant walking away from leading the organization.

Reliance Life Sciences lost momentum by about a year because of this issue. Programmes which were delayed had to be put back on track. Morale was low. Some leaders took sides. Two of them questioned my authority. People were playing politics and gossiping. Many were unsure about what would happen to Reliance Life Sciences. Some claimed that we did not have a future. The pessimists among these individuals left. It was hard to quantify the extent of the damage but the damage was done and had to be addressed. Naturally this was stressful for me, but I dealt with the matter without displaying my emotions to my colleagues.

UGLY FACE OF COMPETITION

Along with greater visibility came competition. Market competitors became active. Some of them were not-so-positive and others were downright negative. They were probably smarting from the threat of looming competition in the marketplace or from the fear of losing their key employees to the new kid in town that Reliance Life Sciences was.

Also on the not-so-positive side, we had to deal with doctors who were loyal to our competitors and were not willing to prescribe our products, or use our molecular medicine testing services. Our competitors discreetly released negative reports about us to the media. These stories would either take a pot shot at us or would only present one side of the story. Some competitors would conduct job interviews with our employees with the objective of ferreting out information about Reliance Life Sciences. Our competitors also lobbied regulators and government officials against us. One competitor, who was way behind us in clinical development programmes, went to the extent of promising our potential licensing partners that they would get marketing approval much before Reliance Life Sciences would get it. In reality, the competitor obtained approval much after us.

I can think of many instances of how the ugly face of competition manifested. In one instance, a senior bureaucrat in one state government took a decision to invoke our bank guarantee when we had a shortfall in the supply of a product in a government tender. This was done without giving us a fair hearing. When my colleagues met him, he openly made uncharitable remarks about us and called the larger Reliance group names. It is normal for government agencies to face delays in deliveries from suppliers and condone them, if the reason for the delay was genuine and amends were made. But in our case, the bureaucrat acted in vengeance.

Another time, an international generic pharmaceutical company signed a confidential disclosure agreement with us but after going through a due diligence exercise, it summarily said that it was not interested in forging a partnership with us. We realized that this company probably wanted to gain competitive intelligence in the guise of seeking an out-licensing partnership.

We even faced problems with traders of our products. In 2014, during a period of shortage of albumin, some traders, who did not have access to our product and were deprived of the opportunity to illegally sell albumin at a premium, instigated some journalists to write concocted stories about us. Then there was the case of one member of a technical drug approval committee taking his aggression out on Reliance Life Sciences. He sat in judgement on approvals for conducting clinical trials and for marketing, depending on the stage of development. He had a dominating style and would overshadow other members of the committee and the regulatory agency officers. In one particular presentation of clinical trial data, when he could not punch holes in the data analysis, he resorted to making value judgements.

Later, the same person wanted additional data, which was not scientifically required in that context. The objective was clearly to delay Reliance Life Sciences. Fortunately, the data had been captured during the study. We subsequently came to know that he was the coordinating investigator for the clinical trials of the same biosimilar for a big Indian pharmaceutical company. This was clearly a conflict of interest, which I brought to the notice of the regulators.

In another instance, we learned about a company in India that was getting marketing approval for darbepoetin in a bizarre manner. This company had done a clinical trial for their darbepoetin product by comparing it with erythropoietin, an older generation drug. This was like comparing apples and oranges. Erythropoietin has a completely different pharmacological profile compared to darbepoetin. This was against the biosimilar guidelines. More than non-conformance to guidelines, it was scientifically unacceptable. Nowhere in the world would such data merit approval. I flagged this to the regulators but to no avail. We also had some overseas doctors refusing to try our product, which had gone through clinical trials and regulatory approval. They did this on the flimsy grounds that it was an Indian product.

As a result of such disabling actions, we have had to contend with delays in development, slower market traction for new launches, financial write-offs, and above all, facing flak within the Reliance group for undue delays.

Any new entrant, from a company, community or country, has to be prepared to face such situations and appropriately deal with them. In my experience, the best way is to communicate with the right constituencies. Continue to focus on objectives quietly, reinforce strengths and address weaknesses. Above all, it is imperative to have the resolve to overcome setbacks. It is also prudent to have good financial provisioning. You may end up posting lower profits but it helps in the long term, as long as the provisioning by finance leaders does not go overboard out of extreme conservatism or fear.

ENABLERS

In complete contrast, there were many among our constituencies who were positive and supported us, which enabled us to achieve our goals. Their support far outweighed the negative impact of the detractors and gave us confidence. It reinforced our tenacity to develop more and more differentiated products for dire and unmet medical needs.

This positivity manifested in many ways. We had more enquiries for business opportunities in clinical trials, contract manufacturing, principal-to-principal business partnerships, out-licensing and partnerships for our products and technologies. More and more banks were keen to lend to us while vendors and service providers wanted to sell us more. Unsolicited proposals for in-licensing opportunities came up regularly. Venture capital funds wanted us to invest in their biotech funds. Potential acquisitions, media queries, invitations for participating on conference panels came up regularly. Professional organizations also wanted us to join them.

However, visibility had some not-so-desirable features. Requests were made for donations and sponsorships, when we had just started to stand on our feet. Requests for advertisement support came from unrelated quarters and we were pressured to appoint specific distribution partners and hire referred candidates for jobs. We needed to learn how to deal with frustrations and with the ugly face of competition and actions by disablers, and to keep the winning spirit in the organization going and growing.

GOVERNMENT FATIGUE

One cause of frustration was the response from government committees whose members seemed to be fatigued with the frequency of visits by my colleagues, who showed up regularly for all committee meetings. On the other side, these colleagues bore the brunt of facing the review committees.

I would regularly make day visits to Delhi along with Ashok Sonurlekar of the Regulatory Affairs Group. The objective was to discuss with senior regulators, the larger context of our medical products. This was to help create an environment of understanding about what Reliance Life Sciences stood for and to seek the support of the regulators. Ashok has been a great support. He is very conversant with the rules and regulations, and forms and processes related to regulatory approvals, because of his long experience in the industry. He also has both a motivational and moderating effect on me when I feel frustrated with slow progress or pushbacks on approvals. He is older than me and has influenced me in increasing my tolerance for imperfection.

Getting government approvals in a highly regulated industry is an arduous task. There are no timelines for approval processes. Minutes of committee meetings are issued in the public domain, but take time. At Reliance Life Sciences, our growth meant we had more and more products going through pre-clinical and clinical development and marketing approval, which meant they had to move through the circuitous corridors of the government. The longer the corridors, the greater the fatigue and frustrations.

We started featuring regularly on the agenda of several committees. On one occasion, one regulatory committee member asked, 'Are we here only to review proposals from Reliance Life Sciences?' Undeterred by these comments, we patiently and resiliently followed up with committee members, taking pushbacks and delays on flimsy grounds in our stride. After all, our investments and jobs were at stake.

INTERNAL PUSHBACKS

Reliance Life Sciences also had to deal with internal bureaucracy which originated in the larger Reliance group. It often took a long time to get simple things attended to or resolved and we were often displeased with decisions made by the group. Vendor invoices would get lost and nobody would take responsibility for them, but we had to face the music from irate members. The worst was when we wanted to do something new but got neither a positive nor a negative answer to our requests. It was unnerving. And I have had to face such situations many times. We were left wondering if we had brought up something stupid or touched a raw nerve. I can recall several situations where I have not had a decision from the Reliance group. In one instance, we wanted to set up an overseas office to grow a particular business, but got no response. This put me in a dilemma: should we or should we not go ahead with the plan? In the Indian context, silence or no response can be considered a sign of approval. However, in this case silence was not a sanction. After a period of waiting, we decided to play it safe and tactically withdrew our plans. In another situation, a team member with good standing in the Reliance group wanted to appoint a clearing and forwarding agency, which was inconsistent with policy. I decided to seek consent for the request even though I had valid grounds to reject it. There was no response from the Reliance group.

In a third instance, the Reliance group was giving a big chunk of conference sponsorship to a leading neurologist in Mumbai without us being in the picture. In our view, the doctor and event did not deserve the munificence. I conveyed our point of view to the group leadership, but did not get a response. Thus, Reliance Life Sciences could not benefit from the group's association with this doctor.

After spending so many years in Reliance, I still have to reconcile to these situations. I am open to differing views and I do reconsider my decisions based on compelling reasons. If I have not thought of something, or not seen aspects from the point of view of the other individual or group concerned, I try to correct myself. When I do not get a response, I do try to press for a decision up to a point and then let it go. I then take action based on what is in the best interest of the customer and the organization.

MOTIVATION

An organization needs motivation to perform. A social organization is motivated by the change that it enables in society, while a business is motivated by the contributions it makes to the economy and society. Motivation comes largely from within and, to a lesser extent, from the external world. For corporates, the internal motivation has to be more powerful than the external. This could be in the form of:

- An unfailing conviction in the larger purpose of business.
- The spirit of collective effort.
- Seeing initiatives being successful.
- Being responsible for the accomplishments of colleagues.

- A customer win.
- A deal closed well.
- A winning tender bid.
- A successful audit.
- A legal conflict closed successfully.
- Excellent clinical data.
- A regulatory milestone achieved.
- An organization-supported PhD programme completed.

At a personal level, internal motivation has to be strong. Satisfaction in placing the company above individual aspirations, comfort with not having compromised long-term benefits for short-term gains, and letting one's work speak for itself instead of resorting to raising one's public profile. External motivation is undoubtedly mood-elevating but should not lead to being immodest and having a false sense of pride.

For Reliance Life Sciences, motivation undoubtedly comes from enablers from the Reliance group, from forward-looking regulators and well-wishers. However, a dominant form of motivation comes from patients and doctors:

- Patients being saved from the jaws of death, as with our emergency care tissue plasminogen activators.
- Patients getting back to stability, as with our albumin and immunoglobulin plasma protein products.
- Patients having improved vision with limbal and conjunctival stem cell therapies.
- Patients with chronic wounds being successfully treated.
- Patients with foot ulcers being saved from amputation with a range of advanced wound management products.
- Patients in surgery with heavy bleeding stopped with fibrin sealants.
- Patients with rare cancers diagnosed with a range of oncology markers in molecular medicine, paving the way for purpose-driven therapies.
- Patients with several cancers benefiting from our

biopharmaceuticals and second-generation generic pharmaceutical products.

Specialist and super-specialist doctors are an important constituency among motivators. Every time they report a positive outcome, our teams get motivated. Sometimes, large hospital chains want us to develop specific products. Typically these are products in short supply, irregular supply or are in a monopolistic market situation. We pursue the development of several products arising out of such requests, for example, the hyper-immunes range of products in plasma proteins.

Progressive regulators are also motivators. These are officials who understand the range and scale of the differentiated research, development, manufacturing and marketing engagements of Reliance Life Sciences. Several successive drugs controller generals of India and their colleagues, as well as state drug regulators, constitute this group. I have often interacted with these officials. Their message is clear. 'You people are doing good work. We are with you. Do not be bogged down by the system of governance we have in India.' Their message is emphatic, urging us to develop more products at competitive prices without compromising safety, efficacy and quality; and encouraging us to explore new frontiers in biopharmaceutical development and marketing.

Nikhil Meswani, a director on the board of Reliance Industries Limited, has been another great source of motivation for us. He is an energetic person with a lot of positive energy, and whenever I have gone to him for help, he has been unfailingly forthcoming and, above all, graceful. I have had a similar experience with other senior colleagues in the Reliance system: P.M.S. Prasad, who heads the oil and gas and refining business and provides unstinting support. I have great admiration for his ability to overcome all odds and work assiduously; Kamal Nanavaty, a former colleague from IPCL and head of the polymers business, constantly encourages me by saying, 'You guys are doing great work. Keep it going!' He once told me, 'KV, how is it that you managed to get so much funding from Mukesh Ambani when I am struggling to get money for a technology development centre.' I replied, 'Frankly, I have no idea.' And I still don't know why we got the funding.

Rabindra (Rabi) Satpathy, who came on board Reliance Industries Limited to incubate and lead the solar energy business, was a person with whom I not only shared my frustrations but also became part of his frustrations. Together, we were involved in developing this alternative energy business plan. This was at a time when the regulatory environment had not yet warmed up to the idea of alternative energy and the internal environment in the Reliance group had not delved deep into these new areas. My role was to facilitate and support not only solar energy, but also fuel cells and semiconductors with other groups. Also, with my background in corporate business development and biofuels, I was chosen to support this next-generation business. Mukesh Ambani was sensitive to the multi-billion dollar opportunities in alternative energy and materials. But the hard-nosed finance leads were not on board.

Together, Rabi and I would meet the developers and operators of solar energy devices in India and other parts of the world. This covered the entire value chain from silicon, wafers, cells, and modules to power generation stations, small and large. We would also go with Sudarshan Srinivas into the rural hinterlands to understand the electricity needs of the villagers. We became sensitive to the ground realities and challenges. The group led by Rabi had commissioned a small solar modules plant and a 5 MW solar power plant in Rajasthan. Rabi left the Reliance group when he did not see traction.

There were many other leaders in the Reliance group who helped and supported us. Their dedication was an inspiration for me and many colleagues. Sanjay Mashruwala, managing director of Reliance Jio, the 4G wireless broadband initiative, is one such individual. He is highly talented in project execution, keeps a low profile and deals with all the implementation issues on the ground with a balanced approach. B. Narayan, head of capital procurement and highly skilled in negotiations, supported us in the life sciences campus creation. A.G. Dawda, a construction specialist, responsible for the Jamnagar complex, combined the rare skills of conceptual level thinking and ground execution. His involvement helped us a great deal in getting the life sciences campus completed. All these individuals kept our spirits up and provided us with rock-solid support.

BENEFACTORS

My experience has taught me that behind every successful venture and accomplishment, there are angels and benefactors at work. These could be parents, siblings, other family members, or friends and colleagues. Sometimes even strangers can be benefactors. In the summer of 1980, when I was doing a market survey for anti-corrosive paints for British Paints, I met an executive in Larsen & Toubro. On his own accord, he referred me to a marine paint technologist who gave me valuable insights into anti-corrosive marine paints. My senior colleagues in British Paints were incredulous when I told them about the information I had gathered.

7

CULTIVATING CHARACTER

'Nurturing a cultural ecosystem
lends character to a business.'

The scale-up phase of an organization is among the most demanding periods for leadership. There are stresses at personal and organizational levels. At the personal level are work-life balance and the emotional quotient, with company matters needing intensive engagement. At the organizational level are constraints on working capital, commensurate with the needs of business growth, competing demands for resources, small mistakes potentially having a large impact and delays in programmes and projects, and regulatory approvals being expensive.

The scale-up phase is also a period when the character of a company is shaped, to a larger extent by its corporate culture. Unless it is carefully fostered and consistently reinforced, the organization can end up having an inappropriate generic culture and incongruous domain-specific sub-cultures. The price that the organization can end up paying can be huge, more so in such aspects as quality, costs and shared responsibilities.

SCALING-UP

Reliance Life Sciences started to scale-up on several dimensions from the year 2009. For one, it pursued greater engagements in business domains and new initiatives. This included specialty plasma proteins, a wider range of monoclonal antibodies, oncology injectables, companion diagnostics, advanced wound management products and cosmetic surgical products. Within each of these domains, we worked on a larger portfolio of products. In manufacturing, in order to keep pace with product and market growth, we invested in new facilities. We modified facility configurations for greater flexibility. We invested incrementally, in balancing equipment or production suites, to have expansion in capacities disproportionate to the investment.

PAIN WITH SCALE

It is said, 'Uneasy lies the head that wears the crown', and this is especially true for a CEO of a startup research, development and growth-driven company in a scale-up mode. The challenge of creating and building in a technology domain is undoubtedly exciting. But the flip side is the tremendous demands that it makes on work life, family life and on the emotive quotient, more so if children in the family are at the adolescent stage. What keeps you going in the face of adversity, is the moral commitment to leadership that you signed up for when you had nothing to show in the company, the excitement with every new milestone that you reach, and above all, the satisfaction you get from the larger social engagement, particularly the benefits to the needy.

FOSTERING DISTINCT CULTURES

Inevitably, such growth presented several major and minor

challenges. While we focused on addressing these challenges, we worked on fostering an overarching generic culture across the organization with several sub-cultures at functional levels. This generic culture has several features—openness, transparency, teamwork and consensus-based decision-making. Supplementing this is a management system that encourages and enables performance, quality, safety, environment sensitivity and audits.

Several principles are held high—patients' interests first, conformance to standard operating procedures as a way of life, process innovation on par with product innovation, aggressive cost-competitiveness, value for resources, shared-learning, consensus-based decisions, mutual respect and good behaviour, and electronic systems and processes for transparency and traceability.

At the functional levels, the distinctive sub-cultures are in research, marketing, manufacturing, clinical research, human resources and finance. Research is conducted in a culture of directed creativity. Clinical research has a strong patient interest and compliance culture. Manufacturing is undertaken by an orderly standard operating process in a tightly controlled environment. Marketing flourishes in a culture of camaraderie and a performance-driven incentivized system. Talent development and engagement have become the ethos of human resources, given the scarcity of competent resources. Finance works with a culture of supporting development, while ensuring that resources are optimized and creativity is not stifled.

In marketing, the product-market context of Reliance Life Sciences is very different from that of our parent organization. Today, we are being recognized as a growing niche entity in the biotechnology domain and are in competition with established global, pharmaceutical companies. Our customers are specialized and well-informed doctors who make the crucial decisions for patients. And our research-driven differentiated products make the difference between life and death for patients.

In contrast, in the larger Reliance group, the generic culture is characterized by strong project management, manufacturing excellence and strong financial controls. The financial control culture tends to dominate all other cultures. Reliance group sub-cultures cover the traditional aspects of manufacturing, business and functional support areas. This is not surprising given that the Reliance group of companies has been built on the hydrocarbon-driven energy and materials value chain.

However, once the Reliance group made a foray into organized retail and fourth generation pan-India wireless broadband initiatives, it has had to foster and support new sub-cultures around consumer orientation, and product and service innovation. If this had not been done, team members joining these two initiatives would have had to come to terms with the strong project management, manufacturing excellence and financial controls culture.

For Reliance Life Sciences, developing these cultures did not happen in a pre-determined manner. They spontaneously developed as the company grew. The task of creating a common organization culture with several underlying sub-cultures engaged a good part of my mental bandwidth and time. I had to constantly communicate with employees and walk the talk. Many of the culture development efforts involved changing mindsets and getting teams to shed past practices.

CULTURE OF CONGRUITY

Getting manufacturing facilities built and started can only be achieved with the convergence of seven key functions in the context of Reliance Life Sciences—projects, procurement, validation, manufacturing, quality management, regulatory affairs and HSE, or health, safety and environment. With several activities happening in each group, frequent conflicts in priorities can be expected. Efforts then need to focus on ensuring that all the individuals involved are clear about their roles and responsibilities, and are on the same wavelength with respect to thoughts and action. This is much like the efforts of a maestro conducting an orchestra.

During the projects phase, there were a host of issues that we had to tackle to get convergence and start commercial manufacturing: Features not envisaged earlier were added by manufacturing, thereby vexing procurement and construction; the qualification of biological loads in clean room areas were not up to the mark, delaying the start; exhibit batches, required to demonstrate consistency, failed because of machine issues, leading to manufacturing and engineering blaming each other; quality control took longer than the anticipated time for method qualification, and many more such teething issues. These situations might have been amplified, had we targeted more than one or two manufacturing facilities to go commercial around the same time.

In the new campus, Reliance Life Sciences had to get several manufacturing facilities commissioned. Fortunately, they were sequenced by default, not by design. This made commercialization manageable. The recombinant proteins drug substance plant was the first to be commissioned in July 2008. Then, it was the turn of the larger plasma fractionation and plasma purification plants in January 2009, followed by the active pharmaceutical ingredients facility in January 2009. An oral solid dosage formulation facility was commissioned in April 2011, and a small fermentation products manufacturing facility in January 2013. Much later, in April 2015, an oncology injectables facility was commissioned. The building of facilities is an ongoing effort and continues even today, along with the creation and management of commensurate infrastructure required for raw utilities, clean room utilities, quality control laboratory and validation equipment.

In the commissioning stage, initially, manufacturing

typically would plod through consistency batches, exhibit batches and, later on, in scale-up. Quality control would take longer than estimated for testing, requiring batches to be on hold for validation. Sometimes, the effort would be held up by delays from vendors and purchase requisitions not being placed in time. All this required patience and an unfailing commitment to timely completion.

Getting manufacturing into higher gear was an equally demanding task. Mistakes made in production were very expensive. Delayed raw materials and consumables, longer processing cycles, batches on hold, failed batches; all these had a huge impact, more so because Reliance Life Sciences was a nascent company.

Above all, marketing would have to come up with good estimates of market demand. This was not easy at the introductory and learning phase of a product's market entry. Mismatches could mean either lost opportunities or excess inventories of products with a limited shelf life. The costs of writing off expired stocks could be damaging.

New dimensions were added to this complexity when the product was in clinical development. The volumes needed for clinical trials were small and there could be a long wait for regulatory inspections and manufacturing approvals. The situation got even more complex given the range of products being developed and produced in the facility. There was also the inherent challenge of ensuring that the processes developed in research laboratories were effectively communicated, executed and scaled up at the batch manufacturing level.

Reliance Life Sciences did struggle to get its act together on all these issues. What was needed was a culture of convergence among disparate groups. The chain is only as strong as its weakest link.

CULTURE OF REVIEWS

An effective method that was employed to keep a close check on manufacturing was to have daily review meetings. Reliance Life Sciences first introduced daily reviews for the pilot scale plasma proteins facility in Mumbai, which went on line in 2005. During the review meetings, manufacturing would provide a heads-up on all aspects of its operations. In later years, this responsibility was given to Sasi Kumar, head of planning and control, plasma proteins. To his credit, Sasi does this admirably to this date, and has graduated to head the critical function of plasma sourcing.

Daily reviews, for both my colleagues and myself, are a rather taxing system. The meetings would take place even in my absence and I would get a report. On many days, I could sense the discomfort in the room, but to everyone's credit, they appreciated the value of these meetings in nailing down issues. The reviews did help get everyone involved into a day-by-day task identification and closure mindset. These reviews focused on identifying problems as they happened, as opposed to performing post-mortems after the problems had caused issues or failures. Daily reviews for the plasma proteins business, given its complexity within the biological domain, continue to date.

Subsequently, marketing had to rise to the occasion of promoting more products, achieving higher volumes and streamlining existing processes. We initiated daily reviews for marketing as well. Key operational decisions would be taken at these meetings. Most of the time, these decisions would be related to the tactical aspects of pricing in response to competitor activity, credit, business associate appointments and logistic issues. Later we instituted a mobile phone-based reporting system. This was an information system that was linked to mobile phone-based daily reporting on several parameters. Compliance aspects, combined with field sales force performance were added later. One day, at a daily evening marketing review meeting, S. Venkatesh, head of marketing, asked me if I could do away with this system. He said he was committed to delivering on targets month after month and would be accountable for them. I had no hesitation in agreeing to his request and Venkatesh did deliver on his commitment.

For those who came from organizations where the managing system was liberal, daily reviews were an irritant and were associated with a high level of control and a boss who was breathing down your neck. But you had to see them in the context of an evolving organization. We had to learn through actions since we did not have godfathers to guide us and direct the convergence of diverse disciplines in a purposeful way.

PERIODIC PROGRESS REPORTS

The management review processes that I introduced for better decision-making and control included daily reviews in critical areas, such as plasma proteins, marketing, and facilities nearing completion, and weekly reviews of all activity domains. Additionally, monthly management team meetings were held on a fixed day of the month and periodic reviews were held when required.

Every group head reporting to me had to write two fortnightly reports every month. Based on this, I would send Mukesh Ambani a consolidated fortnightly report. On the first day of every month, I would send him the monthly life sciences report. This report included a presentation covering achievements in the previous month and the agenda for the current month. Preparing these reports and sending them on the very first working day of every month was like second nature to me.

Rama Prasad, head of finance and commercial, has been a great support in achieving and maintaining this discipline. He would have the monthly management information system numbers ready, after having reviewed the numbers with all business heads. The report would contain profit and loss statements for the company as a whole and for each line of business. It gauged the month and year to date actuals against budgets. It covered revenues, costs, earnings, foreign exchange gains or losses, and net profit. In addition, it would look at the following month's performance budgeted parameters and the booked orders position.

Writing these reports also provided an opportunity to introspect on what was going right, what was not going right and what we needed to do to improve. Fortnightly reports were like a mirror showing me how we looked through hard numbers.

CULTURE OF CONSENSUS-BASED DECISION-MAKING

Developing and implementing this management review system kept all of us in the leadership team on our toes. Participation in the weekly meetings was open to all members of the team under review. Presentations would be made on specific aspects. This helped everyone to understand the broader perspectives. In the process, it contributed to their overall development. It moved them away from being fish in a small pond to exploring the ocean. It helped them understand and appreciate other functions and individuals.

The management review meetings helped me to communicate, engage with, joke and use crazy analogies to drive home my point. It helped the group to discuss and debate issues, and take decisions in harmony. I was able to acquire a fair understanding of the strengths and weaknesses of each team member and a sense of respect for what they did. During most meetings, we would engage in light banter on topics ranging from movies to politics, before we got down to business. This helped to break the monotony, lighten the mood and create a culture of consensus-based decision-making.

CULTURE OF SHARED LEARNING

While the participative style of management brought about a culture of consensus-based and democratic decision-making, it also encouraged shared learning. A good part of my learning in this business came through these meetings.

The science folks had a wonderful system of journal club meetings. Dr Venkata Ramana instituted these meetings in Reliance Life Sciences and continues to hold them to date. At these meetings, each team member presents a scientific development or speaks on a topic. These presentations are open to members of other groups too.

Looking at the success of these journal clubs, we thought why restrict them to science, why not have them in non-science areas too? Thus, we instituted journal clubs in all areas. Initially, making a presentation was voluntary, but when I found that a large number of people in the management team were giving it a miss, I made it mandatory for each management team member to make at least one journal club presentation per quarter. They did so grudgingly. We changed the frequency from once a quarter to once in four months, after conducting an opinion poll among the seventy odd management team members. But it remained mandatory.

Journal clubs, tool room talks, monthly management team meetings, status update presentations, weekly reviews and monthly retreats helped bring about a culture of shared learning. These were not as intensive as one would like them to be, but they helped build a knowledge-based organization.

CULTURE OF CLEANLINESS

My interactions with my counterparts in other countries taught me the need to have a campus that reflects the culture of a cleanliness-oriented organization. This was also necessary, given that our manufacturing facilities were all in clean room environments built to different specifications, ranging from Class 100,000 to Class 100.

My obsession for cleanliness and order dates back to my childhood when these habits were ingrained in me and my brothers, by my parents. The biggest challenge was to get these habits ingrained in my colleagues on campus. I have a number of bugbears when it comes to cleanliness—a spot on the wall, an exposed electrical wire in a conduit, a disorderly scrapyard, paper lying on the floor, a dirty rear of an electrical control panel, laboratory coats lying on chairs instead of hanging on hangers, untidy work benches, stack of files in offices—these are just some of the issues that would attract my attention and prompt corrective action.

It took me several site tours and constant communication to get cleanliness and orderliness embedded in the minds of my colleagues. Several members of the leadership team would conduct surprise tours of the various facilities on the Reliance Life Sciences campus, often at night. They would identify cleanliness, operational or procedural non-compliance issues and send out a report. I would review each of these reports and intervene as required. Our persistent focus on cleanliness and operational conformance has caused a fundamental shift in the mindset of many employees at Reliance Life Sciences.

We spend a large sum of money every month on housekeeping, and maintain a large housekeeping staff. But, it is worth it. Many of our visitors, ranging from bright and curious schoolchildren to demanding external auditors, have appreciated the Reliance Life Sciences campus. Credit for this goes to the employees at Reliance Life Sciences who develop, maintain and showcase our facilities.

CULTURE OF AUDITS

The biotechnology-based life sciences business is enveloped in a culture of audits. These audits are conducted by regulators, accreditation agencies, sponsors of clinical trials, contract manufacturing clients, contract research clients, co-marketing partners and licensing partners. The head of quality assurance is the leader of the team from the auditee's side in responding to the auditors. Other functional heads who support the quality assurance head typically included production, engineering, quality control, regulatory affairs, materials, stores, marketing and administration.

Audits always cause anxiety, bordering on tension. They are akin to preparing for an examination. Much worse, it is analogous to an Indian wedding. Things appear disorganized initially, but they fall into place in the end. This happens with unfailing regularity. In the early years, I would personally review almost every aspect of our business before an audit. Later, I delegated this task to group heads and intervened only at the request of a group head. Much later, our pre-audit practice evolved to a level where I would simply be informed of the outcome at the end of the audit or during the weekly review meetings.

On the business side, we were subject to routine financial audits as well as audits by indirect taxation authorities. One added dimension was the legal compliance audit, which was conducted by the legal compliance cell of the Reliance group. We would unfailingly come up unblemished in such audits.

The culture of audits at Reliance Life Sciences has instilled a great deal of confidence in my colleagues, who were able to meet the high standards of independent regulators. It gave me the assurance that we were not doing anything fundamentally wrong. I could go on a vacation and not worry about compliances.

However, as is the case with any highly regulated industry, there were times when Reliance Life Sciences did not live up to the expectations of demanding external auditors. However, we were quickly able to not only demonstrate commitment to remedy the situation, but did it in quick time. For us, every suggestion for improvement or deficiency, however minor, is an opportunity to step up quality standards in our quest for absolute quality.

One audit where we did not do well remains etched in my mind. It was an audit of the recombinant proteins plant by a fairly large global pharmaceutical company for contract manufacturing in September 2011. I reported the outcome of the audit to Mukesh Ambani and he hauled me over the coals. He wanted us to have global best quality systems and processes and leave no stone unturned to achieve this. He was satisfied when we received an approval after we addressed non-compliance issues.

QUALITY MINDSET

This brings me to the struggle that we went through in ingraining a culture of quality across the organization. In the business that we are in, quality is sacrosanct, particularly because our products are used by people who are sick or infirm or suffering from a serious disorder. Not to mention the anxiety, depression and tension that they and their family members go through. Moreover, most of the products we make are either infused or injected into the body. For most of these patients, who are typically in a critical condition in a hospital's intensive care unit, the medical care they receive is more than merely a relief or a cure, but a question of life and death. For family members, medical care means huge costs and the possibility of an uncertain future for the breadwinner. Good medical care gives the doctor the satisfaction of helping a patient and building a reputation. This applies to the hospital too.

This does not mean that quality control is not required in other industries. It matters in every industry, every sector and every product or service. I can think of several examples where poor quality has had a negative outcome:

- Allergies from using cosmetic or washing products.
- Automobiles subject to accidents due to quality issues.
- Food outlets with poor hygiene standards that expose patrons to the risk of food poisoning leading to diarrhoea, 'Delhi Belly', etc.
- Genetically-engineered seeds not giving promised outcomes.
- Pesticides that are ineffective against crop diseases.
- Software crashing resulting in wasting long hours of effort and work.

I have had a penchant for quality control since the eighties, taking up quality issues involving product quality, service levels or the behaviour of company employees. In the eighties and early nineties, I would write a polite letter to the highest levels of the organization concerned, whether it was a multinational company, an Indian company, small-scale unit, neighbourhood shop, or government organization. Since then, it has been through emails. There are no holy cows for me; the high levels at which some of these companies rank on the quality perception rankings does not matter to me. What matters is the experience I have had.

I have had issues with a wide range of products and services —soaps, toothpastes, incense sticks, airlines, automobiles, utilities, food and beverages and banks. The issues that I have faced ranged from brittle soaps and detergents, tube colour ingress into toothpastes, incense sticks that would just not burn, wrong service attitudes of airline crew, fungus in the bread on a flight, and recurring maintenance problems with my car, to ATMs that would throw back your debit card without dispensing money.

I would spare no one, even the managements of companies I had previously had a good experience with. I would be persistent till the issue I had raised was resolved to my satisfaction. At the outset, I would make it clear that my intention was not to undermine the organization in the public eye, but to highlight a quality problem that I had faced, and to ensure that the organization addressed it. I would invariably mark a copy to the top echelons of the organization. I would also write an email to the same individuals to appreciate good products or services.

Reactions would range from a prompt response and redress, to the promise of a response, delayed action or no response at all. If there was delayed action or no response at all, I would simply stop using the company's products or services. I would then spread the word about my experience with that particular company. Since it is not always possible to stay away from a particular organization, such as a monopoly provider, whether a private organization or government agency, I have sometimes had to adopt an attitude of 'grin and bear it' or rather 'crib and live with it'.

In the world of quality, there are no holy cows. Multinational companies give an impression that they stand for quality. My experience has been rather different. At the other end, are government organizations; the word 'quality' does not seem to exist in their vocabulary. Somehow, government organizations in India believe that nothing can happen to them and that they are rulers and not service providers. On the other hand, neighbourhood shops are very good at responding to quality issues, typically replacing the product in question without any questions being asked.

CULTURE OF QUALITY

I wanted Reliance Life Sciences to be paranoid about quality. Every aspect mattered—the quality of people, products, services, materials, customer services, infrastructure, construction, manufacturing facilities, laboratories, maintenance, training, systems, processes, communications, work environment, food, campus life and support services.

I leave no stone unturned when it comes to quality delivery. If an issue is flagged to me by colleagues or customers, I will follow through to its logical end. I state clearly that the customer must get the benefit of doubt even if you think that there is no issue. Prompt response and communication with the customer is important.

A divisional railway manager of the Baroda division of Indian Railways once wrote to me. I had raised an issue about the state of railway compartments. He responded tersely that we get what we deserve. If we do not demand, we do not get. I often communicate this to employees, and goad colleagues, family members and friends to write and demand quality from companies.

However, at Reliance Life Sciences, getting quality entrenched in the minds of team members, who come from different backgrounds and have varying attitudes, was a challenge. We opted for a 'Quality Everywhere' initiative, an enterprise-wide effort that embraced virtually all aspects of quality and involved a large number of employees. To achieve this, we formed several sub-committees with specific charters. These sub-committees reported to an apex committee. The apex committee meetings, attended by all sub-committee heads, would be chaired by me. These teams would formulate the charter, objectives, strategies and action plans for their respective quality sub-committees. They got initiatives off the ground and oversaw their implementation. The sub-committees would meet regularly and the apex committee once a quarter. Dr Arnab Kapat has been leading this effort.

Alongside this, were a number of communication initiatives: a 'Quality Everywhere' logo, whose design was finalized after soliciting entries from all employees; journal club presentations; tool room talks; and email communications along with my own presentations for the monthly retreats.

All these initiatives resulted in a string of approvals from regulators from highly regulated nations. In early 2016, we received USFDA approval for our active pharmaceutical injectable manufacturing plant. This was a big motivator for the team. Highly regulated country approvals were not new to Reliance Life Sciences. The clinical research business had received three USFDA approvals earlier. These were for studies done for clients who made US product dossier submissions for marketing authorization. The biopharmaceutical and pharmaceutical plants had European approvals.

The USFDA plant approval was special in the context of the Indian pharmaceutical industry, which had seen a series of USFDA warnings and product bans over data manipulation, unkempt facilities, denials, hindering audit and lack of transparency and traceability. Reliance Life Sciences had received some positive media coverage contrasting our approval with the plethora of warnings and bans faced by many companies in the Indian pharmaceutical industry. However, the approval placed a greater onus on us to uphold quality at all times and in every area of our operations.

I believe that quality is a journey and not a destination, and I would communicate this message to my colleagues. There is no perfect standard when it comes to quality since the objective is to do better and better as part of a continuum. This is why the prefix 'c' is used in cGMP denoting current Good Manufacturing Practices, spelt out by regulators for pharmaceutical standards. These range from Good Laboratory Practices (GLP), Good Manufacturing Practices (GMP), Good Tissue Practices (GTP), Good Automated Manufacturing Practices (GAMP), Good Distribution Practices (GDP), Good Clinical Practices (GCP), and so on.

Our efforts in continually raising quality standards have to be unrelenting.

CULTURE OF SAFETY

As with quality, I am concerned about safety. Somehow in India, we are not safety-conscious. Consequently, we do not demand safety. You see unsafe acts and unsafe conditions everywhere. Potholed roads cause accidents and death. Construction sites lack personal safety equipment for workers, so accidents are common. Oil spills are not cleaned and cause skids and falls. Lack of footpaths in many areas lead to pedestrians and vehicles vying for the same stretch of road. Vehicles parked on footpaths and vendors selling their wares on them forcing pedestrians to walk on the road. Vehicles being driven in the wrong direction. Open drains. Jaywalking by pedestrians. Motorcycle Romeos speeding—need I say more?

We determined that this mindset needs to be changed as far as the Reliance Life Sciences campus is concerned and began an enterprise-wide initiative focusing on every aspect of safety—personal safety, manufacturing processes, infrastructure such as roads within the campus, floors and stairs, contractor safety measures at construction sites, emergency preparedness and response, etc. As with quality, we made a concerted effort in the area of safety. Safety was inculcated as a line responsibility. Several sub-committees involving a large number of employees and an apex committee were instituted. The focus was on communication, with a strong commitment from the leadership team to share learning and experiences.

Through this safety initiative, Reliance Life Sciences has been able to reduce safety incidents to virtually zero. Interestingly, many employees have utilized the safety lessons learned at Reliance Life Sciences to make their neighbourhoods and home environments safe for their near and dear ones.

CULTURE OF ENVIRONMENT SENSITIVITY

The same sensitivity is needed for dealing with the environment and with Mother Nature. There is evidence all around us about the way we have messed up the environment:

- Rampant use of environment-unfriendly materials.
- Blatantly polluting automobiles.
- Perfunctory non-polluting certificates given to vehicles by wayside establishments.
- Disorganized waste disposal, including street littering and garbage lying uncollected for long periods.

However, I must say winds of change are visible with the younger generation becoming more sensitive to environmental issues.

At Reliance Life Sciences, we resolved to move to an environment-friendly campus, which meant an enterprise-wide initiative on sensitivity to the environment, initiating proactive measures and good communications. In this domain, the focus was on materials, packing, use of paper, treatment of effluents, bio-waste, other types of waste, pollution control, and so on.

As with safety, our environment sensitive attitude has encouraged employees to develop environment consciousness in their homes and with their near and dear ones. The environmental effort has been led by Neha Bhende.

CULTURE OF ELECTRONIC OFFICE

One of the spin-offs of our environmental efforts has been the dramatic reduction of paper. The life sciences industry, like many others, relies heavily on documentation in the form of research notebooks, batch manufacturing records, quality analysis certificates, equipment logs, pre-clinical and clinical study records, regulatory submissions, etc. Documentation records also have to be maintained for periods specified by country-specific regulations, and we need fire-resistant documentation rooms which take up space and cost money.

Additionally, drug regulators in India want a number of copies for submissions, and some committees want both CDs and physical documents. In contrast, drug regulators in highly-regulated countries insist on online submissions. To the credit of Indian drug regulators, there has been a gradual shift to electronic records, and more changes are on the anvil, allowing a number of submissions to be made electronically through computer networks. However, paper is expected to remain a necessity in our operations.

Reducing the use of paper was just the first step in Reliance Life Sciences's electronic office initiative; it helped in enabling traceability and preventing data manipulation. In March 2013, after consulting colleagues, I decided to make Reliance Life Sciences fully electronic. As a first step, I announced that team members were no longer required to bring paper, pads and diaries to meetings. They could make notes on their laptops or mobile phones. We also stopped buying writing pads, and I made sure my office and my desk, were free of paper.

We looked at virtually every aspect that could be electronically enabled and identified nine technology platforms for this purpose. These included a laboratory implementation management system, quality assurance management system, electronic batch manufacturing records, electronic research notebooks, electronic office, documentation management system, warehouse management system, visitor management system and an enhanced customer relationship management system. All these electronic technology platforms were taken up for implementation in phases. Except for electronic batch manufacturing record, warehouse management system and the enhanced customer relationship management system, all the other platforms were implemented by December 2015 in phase 1. We then took up other aspects, such as getting research laboratory instruments to communicate with the electronic platforms, and made this a criterion for new equipment purchases.

Making Reliance Life Sciences fully electronic involved several challenges associated with technology competencies, hardware, network infrastructure, software, data storage, implementation and training. When the electronic office was being implemented, I mandated that any request or communication coming to my office should be through the system or by email, and that from 15 January 2015, I would refuse to respond to any communication on paper, except for legal and statutory documents. In one instance, I tore up the paper brought by a colleague for approval to send out the message that I was serious about the electronic office.

My information technology colleagues tended to look for a tool first, in the form of software, and then tried to use the tool, much like a carpenter having a hammer and looking for all the things that can be hammered—from nails to nuts! They did this despite being taught at premier institutes to first understand concepts and needs before thinking of management techniques.

In early 2016, I had the opportunity to work with colleagues from Reliance Jio, the fourth generation wireless broadband initiative, on a blood banking management software. Here I was exposed to the concept of developing a product requirement document or PRD first. This document was based on extensive interactions with users, and developing the solution's features, work streams and technology architecture in terms of its principles, integration and layers of platforms, devices, data, applications and communications. Since then, developing a PRD is a must before looking at a technology solution.

Implementation of electronic platforms also involves good financial, commercial and legal support in the long process of negotiations with software companies. Unlike products, some software companies only give licences to use their software and do not sell it. If they sold software as a product, they would have to face scores of class action suits for all the glitch-ridden products that they released. Selling licences also gives them the privilege of selling a product as they develop it and not the final version that can be bought off the shelf, installed and used.

In my experience, the biggest challenge in transforming to

an electronic office lies in changing mindsets. Accepting and conforming to a modern way of working, assigning the best resources to the core team and being extremely meticulous in customization efforts, are important determinants of success in implementation. Frequent communication plays a vital role in implementing change.

CULTURE OF PUNCTUALITY

We also developed a culture of sensitivity to time. Here again, India lags behind other countries, but is slowly getting better. In Reliance Life Sciences, punctuality is important whether it relates to meetings and events, presentations, monthly retreats or invited talks. Our stress on punctuality began with our monthly retreats. Some of our leaders liked to listen to their voices and would go on and on speaking during these retreats, unmindful of the fact that they were eating into the next speaker's slot and disrespecting others' time. The mood in the room would range from boredom to disgust. What these colleagues did not realize was that they were not only depriving subsequent presenters of quality time, but also disconnecting with the audience.

Initially, I used to step in and politely request them to stop. But when this habit persisted, we decided to use a homegrown information technology solution. We call this rather simple system 'Meeting Manager'. In all my travels overseas, I have not seen such a system in use. Speakers have to upload their presentations into the system and the agenda, topic, speaker, start time and end time, and a link to an underlying uploaded presentation of the speaker, will show up on the screen. All that the speaker needs to do is to click on the link. The best part of it is that the Meeting Manager gives a reminder when two minutes of the presentation are left, as well as when the time is up. At the end of the permitted time, instead of rudely shutting down the presentation, it will start a countdown clock.

The Meeting Manager brought about a great deal of sensitivity to punctuality in the company. It helped to begin and end meetings with multiple presentations, within the allotted time.

There is a popular joke in India about the Indian Railways' timetable. It lists the times of the trains, of course, but what this means is that the train may come on time or it may come at any time after the listed time, even on the following day! Indian Standard Time or IST is also called Indian Stretchable Time! When I go to external meetings, especially government meetings, the situation is more or less the same. In such situations, I am not a master of my time. Meetings can happen at any time after the appointed time, sometimes on the next day, or much later or never. The same thing happens at conferences and events. The more rich and famous a person is, the longer you are likely to wait for them. Otherwise, the person will not be perceived to be important. If you arrive on time, you will probably find that the organizers are yet to show up, or the room is scantily filled. Of course, there are exceptions to these situations and personalities. Fortunately, at Reliance Life Sciences we have been reasonably successful with managing time.

Even in the medical profession, I have found that doctors very rarely honour the time of an appointment. The convenient excuse is that the doctor was busy with other patients or attending to an emergency call, or surgery. If you aggregate the number of hours Indians waste at doctors' offices and hospital clinics, you will get a mind-boggling number reflecting a colossal waste of time. The only doctor who, in my opinion, unfailingly honours an appointment is my dentist, Dr Colin de Sa in Mumbai. He is invariably waiting for his patient. He respects his own time, as well as that of others, which is one of the reasons why my family members and I are his loyal patients.

CULTURE OF COST CONTROL

For Reliance Life Sciences, set in a research and development frame, cost control is more like a religion. We could have had runaway costs in the following circumstances:

- A scientist continuing to do research with no tangible outcomes.
- Excess orders being placed, which are inconsistent with optimum requirements, or out of sync with the bills of materials in batch manufacturing.
- Excessive consumption of consumables.
- Filing of provisional patents with no demonstrable results, leading to write-offs.
- Filing of final patents without having the ability or business case for maintaining them in different countries, again leading to write-offs.
- Excessive travel and expense accounts of executives. Relaxed human resource policies on reimbursements of expenses.
- Expensive facilities.
- Equipment grossly underutilized or not utilized.
- Batches failing to make the grade on yields.
- Batches failing on quality.
- Products returning with shelf-life expiry.
- Mismatches between physical and book inventories.
- Expired consumables.
- Uncontrolled hiring.
- Unhedged foreign currency transactions that result in exchange rate losses.

In my experience, the best way to keep costs very tight is to sensitize team members and create a culture of cost ownership and control. This is to be followed by instituting a rigorous system of frequent analysis and periodic review. But above all, the leaders must demonstrate sensitivity to cost, and practice thrift themselves instead of simply pontificating.

At Reliance Life Sciences, the management information system (MIS), published on a weekly basis, indicates the major performance parameters and costs of each business and functional group. This comes out of the SAP database. The MIS report forms the basis of weekly financial and commercial reviews. Periodic reviews with key members of the management team help to constantly focus on identifying the 'fat' in the organization and the methodology to cut the 'fat'.

Due to the capital intensity and higher proportion of material costs in some businesses like plasma proteins, for every dollar of overheads that we incurred, we had to earn two to two and a half times net revenues just to break even. In this endeavour, Reliance Life Sciences faced two challenges. The first challenge resulted from the Reliance group imposing a 'One Reliance' conceptual framework. This framework is conceptually good but did not factor the unique context of Reliance Life Sciences and its evolutionary stage. As a result, the inherent rigidity burdened Reliance Life Sciences with higher costs.

The other challenge was cultural. Team members, who came from academic organizations or from organizations that were rich and prosperous, typically did not look into value for money. To inculcate sensitivity to costs, I often communicated to colleagues that we must spend as if we were spending from our own pockets. I also set a personal example by travelling economy within India, Europe and the US.

CULTURE OF CASH FLOWS

It is said, 'Revenues are vanity, profits are sanity and cash flows are reality'. This statement is very profound. It is relevant to every business organization, particularly a startup company in the capital-intensive, long gestation period that Reliance Life Sciences is in. It is even more relevant when the company starts making profits and improves profitability.

There are several instances where a company can show revenue and revenue growth which do not translate into profits, because of the company's adverse cost structure and costly decisions. There are other examples of companies which have revenues and profits, but do not have cash flows. This is because of weak credit policies, improper credit limits, poor collection records, inconsistent payment policies and excessive investments beyond means. These examples do not reflect deliberate fraud by executives or management, but poor management control policies, systems and processes.

The Reliance group of companies was predominantly shaped in the classical mould of a business model in which revenue streams emanate from an underlying opportunity, leading to a profitable and sustainable business. In the Reliance school of thought, the return of capital to investors and cash flows mattered more than profits. Profits, in turn, mattered more than net revenues. This was certainly not a new concept. But, it manifested in leadership performance being evaluated on cash profits, with shortfalls in revenues being relatively less of a concern.

In Reliance, budgets are only for financial planning and not a sanction to spend. Most newcomers take time to get used to this. For businesses that are constantly on a growth path, where there are competing demands on capital and a drive for capital productivity, spends are regularly monitored and realigned. This is done in a manner that causes the least turbulence, unless the situation warrants it.

As Reliance Life Sciences learned to stand on its own feet from the year 2008, the reality of cash profits and cash flows hit hard. It first showed up in outstanding payments to be received from customers. Marketing was on a scale-up mode. As a result, in their anxiety to drive primary sales, the team became a bit lax with business associates on collections. Vendor payments got delayed. Some vendors put us on advance payments. Some others stopped selling products or services. To add insult to injury, the shared services of the Reliance group kept adding new requirements in vendor invoices. Despite this handicap, we decided to pull our socks up. We resorted to daily reviews of collections. We brought in a system of cheque payment with orders, with the cheque to be deposited on the third day of despatch. With extraordinary marketing efforts, we were able to restore order, and this discipline continues to this day.

We also brought in a weekly review of commitments on purchase orders and work orders during the weekly commercial review meetings. This was to ensure that we were not going overboard on commitment exposures, and that commitments were consistent with activity levels. On the accounts payable side, we had weekly reviews on invoices pending payment, segregated into categories of 'under processing' by shared services, pending due to issues of 'service entries', 'quality control clearance', and 'vendor issues'. In each category, the break-up in terms of ageing, on operational expenses and capital expenditure, was given. This break-up of figures provided greater granularity and helped fix responsibilities for resolving issues.

From April 2014, with recourse to bank loans for capital expenditure, we neared our self-imposed limit. This limit was far lower than the bank's credit limit. We brought about a mandate to all business groups to earn cash to fund their own planned capital expenditure. This meant that the capital expenditure budget would be cleared only for those businesses which had cash profits. Even within these businesses, cash flows would determine actual capital expenditure. Each business had to commit some amount from their cash profits to common cause projects, such as infrastructure and corporate needs. In effect, as CEO, I had to seek capital funding for infrastructure and corporate capital expenditure.

In the process of creating a strong focus on cost control and cash flows, we were able to bring greater fiduciary responsibility among the key leadership. I must say that, in all these endeavours, Rama Prasad as head of finance, provided strong support, and all the members of the core management team responded magnificently. As a result, we ended the financial year 2015-16 with far higher profitability in relation to top line growth, and with strong cash profits. To maintain this level of profitability, Reliance Life Sciences will have to remain steadfast in its commitment to cash profits as well as to revenues.

8

OVERCOMING SETBACKS

'Building a business often involves developing
immunity to impediments.'

*Setbacks often happen in organizations. The larger the scale
of operations, the greater the downside. The greater the market
share and dependency on a product to drive revenues, the
higher the impact of a market downside. The larger the foreign
exchange rate risk exposure, the greater the risks of adverse
external sector changes.*

*For large organizations with strong profits and cash
flows, the damage can probably be digested. But, for smaller
organizations, the stomach for setbacks is weak and varies
depending on the state of evolution and strength of cash flows.*

*But all setbacks hold lessons. If taken in stride in a
constructive manner, they make the organization that much
more robust and resolute. In the end, from every setback, there
is new sustenance.*

BLACKOUT

Here I was at Reliance Life Sciences, at the forefront of the
fight to forge our future, experiencing all the stress and strain

that came from the growth of the company. But I was yet to be tested to my limits. It came one Saturday morning, on 23 March 2013, to be precise. I was recuperating from an uneventful trans-urethral resection of prostrate procedure performed with spinal anaesthesia at a leading private tertiary care hospital in Mumbai. One day after the surgery when I went to the bathroom to brush my teeth, I started feeling uneasy. That's all I can recall. My wife Saroj was keeping guard outside in the room with the door slightly ajar. The next moment, I realized I was being helped to the chair. I could feel severe pain at the back of my head. I sat down, dazed and pressed my nose to stop it from bleeding. I had apparently had a blackout and struck my head on an iron pipe in the bathroom as I fell.

While I was in the bathroom, the hospital newspaper boy had knocked on the room door to deliver the morning newspaper. Saroj turned to take the newspaper and heard a thud from the bathroom. By the time she picked up the newspaper and looked back, I was lying on the bathroom floor. She had shouted for help and the duty nurses had come rushing to the room. I was helped to the bed and given an icepack to soothe the pain at the back of my head. Saroj insisted that I should get a CT scan done but I refused, claiming with bravado that it was nothing to worry about and I was fine. Throughout that day and the next day, I had to keep ice packs on my head to reduce the pain. Though I have a high tolerance for pain, I found the pain severe, but I did not express how I felt to anyone.

Strangely the nurses on duty did not call for an emergency doctor. Being a weekend, the resident doctors came to review my case, saw me continuing to work on my laptop on the hospital bed and probably thought there was nothing to worry about. I was also on the phone on and off, talking to colleagues about the month's performance. It was the last month of the financial year at Reliance Life Sciences. Our annual financial performance mattered a lot.

Personally, I was keen to get out of the hospital and was looking forward to my scheduled discharge on Monday. On Monday morning, I vomited a little after breakfast. When the urologist's assistant came for a review, I mentioned that I had vomited. He said that it could have been because of acidity caused by the painkillers. He signed for my discharge. I felt good about getting out of medical confinement.

I was discharged at about 11 am and was happy to get home. My aged and bed-ridden mother was happy to see me. I had a shower, said my prayers and had a cup of coffee followed by lunch. Soon after, I vomited everything I had eaten. I had a creepy sense that something was going wrong because of the head injury. But with a sense of bravado, I got down to work on my laptop at the dining table, my preferred work place where I could work, eat, watch television or listen to music, whenever I wanted.

But that day was to be different, and I was unable to do all these things. I soon felt a stiffening in my neck. I spoke to Dr Chaitanya Gulvady at the Reliance Industries Limited head office. He was the medical officer supporting my hospitalization from the Reliance group. He advised me to immediately go to Breach Candy Hospital for a CT scan, and he said that he would be there as well. The hospital was about half the distance from my home to his office. Fortunately, my wife had asked our car driver to wait after we had returned from hospital earlier in the day. We lost no time and rushed to the hospital. I had a lurking fear that something would happen on the way to the hospital and remained silent during the ride.

When we reached Breach Candy, Dr Gulvady was waiting at the imaging centre and had arranged for the doctor there to take me in for an emergency CT scan. After the procedure, the radiologist came out and stood in front of me while Dr Gulvady sat next to me.

I sensed that something was wrong. Dr Gulvady said that I had bleeding in the brain because of the head injury and there was a hairline fracture on the right side of my forehead. I was told by both doctors that nothing could be done as the brain structure was intact. If it was disturbed, I would have needed emergency brain surgery. However, I had to be placed under the observation of a neurologist. I was advised to be re-admitted to the tertiary care hospital I had left that morning.

Obviously I had been experiencing the after-effects of the fall all weekend but my sense of bravado had got the better of me, causing me to ignore my wife's protestations. The hospital was at fault too since the nurses on duty and the resident doctors had either overlooked the fall or were blissfully ignorant about what to do about it. It could well have been that the hospital did not have a standard operating procedure to deal with such situations.

INTERVENTION

I was readmitted to the private tertiary care hospital. The nurses in the ward, who were in the same day shift, were surprised to see me back. Soon after, there was a succession of resident doctors and technicians who came to review my case and conduct tests on me. Among them was the assistant to the neurologist who took me through a number of alertness, memory, sensory and motor function tests. I thought I had done well on all the tests, except for the one in which I had to walk in a straight line.

The neurologist came to see me later that evening. He had reviewed all the reports and told me that I had internal injury and bleeding, but did not require brain surgery. He said all he could do was to put me on oxygen, observe me for a few days and leave it to nature to heal. Higher levels of oxygen, he said, would help with the healing. The bleeding would dry out but I was at a high risk of getting seizures. The only drug to deal with the problem was Clobazam which would suppress brain activity. He said that he was giving me the lowest dose of 5 mg to be taken thrice a day. The other drugs he was giving me addressed my low sodium and vitamin B12 levels (common with vegetarians).

My son called from Houston to ask about my recovery after the surgery. I told him that there was no cause for alarm, that I would get home soon and that he should get on with his work. He continued to call twice a day and wanted to talk to me, not satisfied with what my wife told him about my condition.

Then an intensivist, a critical care physician, came to see me. He said he would monitor my electrolyte levels, which could have caused the blackout. During those days, while I lay in the hospital bed on medical oxygen, I realized the value of oxygen not just as a life support but as a therapeutic molecule. This is analogous to cash flows in business. Both oxygen and cash flows are life supporting, acting as therapeutics in healing a sick person or a company, and driving a reasonably healthy company to be more energetic and grow.

As soon as I started feeling better, I told my wife that the worst was over. I wanted to get out of the hospital and go back to work. I had decided to fight it out and get back on my feet; be as active as ever. She would have none of this and wanted me to stay in hospital as long as it was medically required. By nature, I cannot sit idle. And, I wanted to keep my mind fertile and active.

RECOVERY

Over the next few days, I got as busy as I used to be, even though I was in hospital. I worked on my emails, notes and reports and had conference calls with my colleagues, since the financial year ending was drawing to a close. Several colleagues and well-wishers came to see me. What touched me was their concern and affection. Mukesh Ambani called me to ask if I was fine. I said I was. Whenever he called me to ask what was happening at life sciences, my instinctive response would be the same—one word 'Fine' followed by a very short brief on our status.

My marketing leadership came up and said, 'You get better, leave the performance aspects to us and we will achieve our targets.' And they did. Nuns from Convent Girls High School, where my wife teaches, came over to my room and conducted a bedside prayer service for my recovery. This moved me, and does so even today whenever I think about it. Most hospitals in India do not stop priests, nuns, imams and monks to offer a prayer service for sick patients—a brilliant comment on India as an open, tolerant and peace-loving society.

Dr Gulvady and other medical doctors from the company called on me regularly. Dr Somnath Banerjee, head of occupational health at Reliance Life Sciences, was a constant source of support. He even stayed overnight at the hospital till my twin brother came down from Hyderabad to support us. The neurologist, I was told, was fed up with the number of doctors who called him to ask about my health and asked my colleague, Dr Chandra Viswanathan, who I was. She told him about me and I believe he replied that I never came across as the head of a company. She told him that I was not made that way.

I kept bugging the intensivist to discharge me. He told me that when the sodium level came up close to the minimum of 135 mmol/L, he would discharge me. My sodium level had gone as low as 100 mmol/L but with treatment, it had come up to 123 mmol/L.

My wife wanted me to stay in the hospital as long as it was required but, I was fed up of being in a cloistered environment. I goaded the intensive care head to let me go and he acquiesced, much to my delight. My mother was equally delighted to see me back home from hospital. She was in the dark about my fall and head injury, and remains unaware of it to this day. I was clear that she was not to be told. I was sensitive to her situation of having lost her youngest son due to a head injury accident that led to a coma. In addition, she had depression and was mostly bedridden. My twin brother had told her that I had had a drug reaction which is why I had to go back to hospital. My wife's mother, who was staying with us, was also unaware of my condition but was told about it later.

DEFIANCE

On the day of my discharge, four days after my readmission to hospital, my neurologist reviewed my case and advised me to rest at home for a week. I was advised a relatively high salt diet. I was allowed to walk to a limited extent inside the house, but someone had to walk alongside me. I couldn't walk outside the house, nor could I exercise or swim, not even in shallow waters, as a precaution against seizures. I learnt that when you have a blackout while in water, it does not matter if the water level is one foot or ten feet deep, your chances of drowning are extremely high. The neurologist told me that he would review my case after a month.

I defied some of the medical advice. We had our monthly retreat a day after I came home from hospital, and I decided to participate. I had never missed a monthly retreat, a tradition since the very inception of Reliance Life Sciences. I wanted to give my customary introduction of new team members and an update on developments at Reliance Life Sciences. My wife would have none of this and wanted me to stay at home. I felt I owed it to my colleagues, particularly my marketing colleagues, who had performed well despite all the challenges during the year, to attend the retreat. They had assured me when I was in hospital that I needn't worry about the company's performance.

I stood my ground and Dr Somnath told my wife that he would take care of me. But she wasn't convinced so she came along with me to the retreat. I was in a 'fragile' state as Mahua Bhattacharya, my colleague and head of corporate communications put it. I was escorted to the podium by Dr

Somnath and received a big round of applause from my colleagues, three hundred of them, at the atrium of the campus building. I had to sit on a high stool that had firm legs, instead of a chair. I completed my address, went to my office, cleared papers and emails, and went home. In the following days, I held meetings at home, listened to lots of music, more than I had listened to in many years, and kept myself very busy intellectually.

OPPORTUNITY IN ADVERSITY

In the first week of April 2013, the annual marketing meet came up. It was being held in Agra, home of the Taj Mahal. I decided to go. My wife said, 'No way.' My brother said, 'Why not.' Being head of Indian Immunologicals Limited, he knew the importance of this marketing meet in the annual calendar. It really meant a lot for motivating and charging up the marketing professionals. Dr Somnath said he would accompany me, but my wife was concerned that I may have a fall in the hotel room. I asked her to come along and to see the Taj. She retorted that her objective would be to look after me and not to see the Taj. I responded that people from all over the world came to see the Taj, so she could do the same thing. Here was an opportunity for us in the aftermath of adversity.

We went to Agra, but unfortunately my mother went into a delirious state the night before we were to take a plane to Delhi en route to Agra. She had been an insulin-dependent diabetic for over twenty years, and had low blood sugar that night. I could recognize the cause of the symptoms and intervened by giving her sugar water and a chocolate. It worked. Soon enough, she recovered. But we were not happy to leave her in the care of nurses for the couple of days that we would be in Agra. I called up my twin brother. He immediately reserved a plane ticket for Mumbai for the following morning, and came home just after we had left for the airport. This is the strength of the family network in India!

One of the principles of action learning of British educationist Prof Reg Revans is, 'In every adversity, there is an opportunity.' My close encounter with death gave me an opportunity to appreciate this more than ever before. It is also true that there is unity in adversity. The determination of my colleagues to perform during that period of uncertainty about my future is a stellar example. They came together as one and posted a 30 per cent increase in revenues and a big improvement in profits, over the previous year.

REALIZATION

It was much later that I realized the magnitude of what I had gone through. My good friend Narasimhan Srinivasan's wife, Dr Veena Vani, a Yale-trained, US-based physician who had specialized in internal medicine, told me that I was fortunate to have survived. My family physician in Mumbai went to the extent of saying that it was a miracle that I had survived. Only then did I get a sense of how close to death I had been.

My wife and son wanted me to take things slow and easy. But I could not slow down my pace since I had an unfinished agenda at Reliance Life Sciences, as well as in life, in general. In fact, I redoubled my efforts and engagement with Reliance Life Sciences. I was soon exploring new areas, such as advanced wound management products, a new range of hyperimmunes and peptides.

BRAIN BIOCHEMISTRY

My fall and head injury and subsequent recovery, led me to some revelations about myself and about nature. I read more about the brain, and was even more fascinated and intrigued by it. Within me, my brain biochemistry had changed. I began talking a lot. My family members, friends and colleagues, who were used to my quiet disposition, found this very strange. At home, I would talk endlessly, especially when my wife and I would walk for about an hour after dinner, which became a daily habit after my doctors allowed me to walk outside with a companion. We have continued this habit to this day.

I became more aggressive when it came to my sense of purpose. This manifested in candid conversations, which was unusual for me given that diplomatic talk had been my preference earlier. I became more demanding about the performance of my colleagues in Reliance Life Sciences. I felt greater emotive connect with the people around me and conversed more with the staff of service provider companies as well as strangers. I became more benevolent and donated for good causes more than ever before. I also developed a greater sense of humour and would crack jokes about myself and about others. I realized that to joke about others, you must first learn to joke about yourself.

AFTER-EFFECTS

After my fall and head injury, I experienced daily headaches on one side of my head or the other, which continue to this day, though with reduced frequency. My blood pressure which was normal before my fall, now fluctuates, but is progressively getting better with higher doses of medication. My nose runs without warning. Sometimes, I shed tears from one eye without any apparent reason. My doctors have told me that these symptoms will normalize over time. Nobody can say when. My sleep cycle is the worst affected. If I get five hours of sleep a day, I am happy. This is in stark contrast to the days before my fall when I used to sleep eight hours a day.

I have lost the ability to smell. My neurologist had told me that if the olfactory nerve, that is responsible for transmitting neurosignals and runs from the top of the nose to the roof of the brain, was completely damaged, I would never get back my sense of smell. If it was partially damaged, I would be able to smell, but the extent of recovery and when it would happen, cannot be predicted. Till today, I cannot smell and have assumed that I am an alien in the world in this regard. Initially I used to feel bad when others around me described an aroma. Later I reconciled myself to this state. I was told that some head injury patients lose both their sense of smell and sense of taste. Thankfully I can taste food, even if I cannot take in the aroma of food. Small mercies!

I continue to fight the physical manifestations of my fall and head injury, while accepting the functional manifestations, to this day.

SETBACKS

This setback to my health has made me see everything from a new perspective in my personal and professional life. It's the same with a company which receives a setback. In the life sciences industry, setbacks can be many: Failed batches, failures in animal studies or clinical trials, potential customers or partners walking away just before deal closure, predatory pricing by competitors or long delays in regulatory approvals.

The larger the scale of operations, the bigger the downside; the longer the batch processing time, as with mammalian cell culture bioreactors, the greater the risks of contamination; the more expensive the animal study or clinical trial, the greater the cost and exposure to failure risks; the greater the number of patients to be accrued in a clinical trial, the longer the duration of the study and timelines for market entry; the greater the market share and dependency on a product to drive revenues, the higher the impact of a market downside of the product, on the organization; the larger the foreign exchange risk rate exposure, the greater the risks of foreign exchange rate changes and the higher the hedging charges.

There are other potential setbacks.

- Issues in validation of facilities.
- Equipment suppliers delaying deliveries inordinately or going slack in support.
- Engineering services' companies getting acquired and offloading the contract to a group company.
- An expert on a review committee for clinical trials or marketing authorization, having a conflict of interest and ragging Reliance Life Sciences' presenters.
- Sudden imposition of a low price or irrational methods for fixing ceiling prices by regulators.
- A key resource preferring to leave the company.

Reliance Life Sciences has faced all these setbacks and more.

FAILURES BEHIND SUCCESS

We had a failure with the first scale-up batch at 2,500 litres of a monoclonal antibody, which is made in a mammalian cell culture reactor. Of all things, a diaphragm valve had given way and there was a sterility failure. The batch had to be scrapped at a high cost. But we learnt from that experience, incorporated changes and later had several successful batches at this scale. I often admire those who run 20,000 litre mammalian cell culture bioreactors. There are very few facilities and few people in the world who run such reactors. One batch failure and a huge loss hits you. A product-based revenue model company can spread the loss over several future batches. But a contract manufacturing company takes a huge hit to its bottom line, as it earns batch-by-batch. This is one reason why contract manufacturing is considered a tough business where only the fittest can survive.

Reliance Life Sciences had a failure with animal studies on a dengue therapeutic that was being developed as a novel protein. We saw good efficacy in the short term with mice.

But longer term survival data was not strong enough. So we stopped the project. Several years of efforts and resources had come to naught. In another instance, after years of development and clinical studies for a biosimilar conducted by a subsidiary company, the European regulators wanted additional data through larger studies. The project went on hold till we could find a partner to share costs and risks.

A vendor of an injectable filling line in an isolator facility ran into problems and walked away from supporting its completion, validation and commissioning. We had to garner support from our engineering team to get the job done. It pushed us back by over a year, but we did not want to have any compliance issues in international regulatory inspections.

With every setback, Reliance Life Sciences has emerged stronger. This has been possible because of a mindset of seeing setbacks as events to deal with in a constructive manner, and with a determination to move ahead with greater resolve. For every success, there are one or more failures. For every successful startup, there are probably hundreds of others in the grave. Over time, society tends to see the success stories not the failed ones.

9

LETTING GO

'Founders cannot cling forever.'

There comes a time when leaders who build an organization ground-up have to let go of their creation, however passionate their involvement may have been. This has to be a process over a relatively defined time. Getting the next line of leadership to take on the mantle is critical. This is easier said than done, because it involves a host of factors—timing, communication, documentation, ensuring enduring policies, systems and processes and having the conviction of longevity of culture, climate and governance. Above all, is the question of right selection of succeeding leaders with vision, maturity and the ability to take the organization to the next level.

Corporate history is replete with examples of the miseries of both individuals and companies who have hung on to each other till they suffocate the company or are mercilessly booted out. A similar fate is met by successful sportspersons and administrators who take far too long or refuse to call it a day.

TIME TO LET GO

Reliance Life Sciences had started to scale up. The foundation of the initiative was falling in place. From the beginning we had envisaged that, at some stage, we would have to focus on scaling up areas that made business sense, and shed or migrate others to the Reliance group. This came about for four initiatives. In a sense, Reliance Life Sciences had become an incubator for a few initiatives for the Reliance group.

However, the separation was painful when it happened, just as it is for parents who have to let go of children when they are old enough to leave home to study, or find their own path in life.

PANGS OF SEPARATION

The first to go was plant tissue culture. It was led by Dr K.S. Murali, a person with passion for tissue culture, landscaping, flora and fauna. When a decision was taken to move plant tissue culture to the Reliance Foundation, Murali left to seek green pastures in the deserts of Oman and is now engaged in agricultural transformation there.

The second was industrial biotechnology. This was led by Dr Vidhya Rangaswamy, who returned from post-doctoral assignments in the US to join us. She operated out of Jamnagar before migrating to the life sciences campus. She developed the first of our fermentation products, before a decision was taken to migrate industrial biotechnology and biofuels to Reliance Industries Limited's Technology Development Centre.

Reliance Life Sciences also nurtured a biofuels initiative, the third initiative to move out of our campus. This initiative, led by Sudarshan Srinivas, banked on turning the 'food versus fuel' debate in the western world, on its head. We believed that food crops could be grown along with fuel crops. This we did by growing fuel crops like 'jatropha' on wastelands, along with food crops. Much later, biofuels migrated to Reliance Industries and Reliance Foundation, and Reliance Industries added the algae-to-oil business route. The experience with farm advocacy for biofuels in Reliance Life Sciences eventually led Sudarshan to conceptualize and roll out the Bharat-India-Jodo (BIJ) initiative at Reliance Foundation. BIJ is the largest and deepest rural development initiative by any single organization.

I had motivated Sudarshan, an exemplary professional working for the National Dairy Development Board, to lead farm advocacy in biofuels. His heart and soul is with the poor in rural India. I often travelled with him to the interiors of several Indian states which brought me constantly in touch with the reality of poverty in the rural hinterland.

Sudarshan is a unique professional. He invested his own money in a small piece of land in a remote Gond tribal village on top of a hill in the Seoni district of Madhya Pradesh state, tucked between Nagpur and Jabalpur. He himself worked on developing barren, rain-fed land and experimenting with crops, all this in order to understand agriculture, hard labour on fields, and what it is to be a poor and marginal farmer.

Sudarshan also regularly has his family members join him in spending weeks staying and working in wastelands in semi-arid, remote and rural areas. He often tells me when I enquire about his well-being, 'I feel like I am on top of the world in rural areas, but like a "manager" in Mumbai.' This is a profound statement. Many corporate organizations and city-bred individuals are hopelessly out of touch with reality. Sudarshan inspired me to motivate my son, Santosh, who is an engineering professional in the US, to have a reality check when he was on vacation in India. The experience enabled Santosh to better understand and appreciate how privileged we all are.

The agro-based food products business was the last one to move out of Reliance Life Sciences. I worked shoulder-to-shoulder with Dnyaneshwar Patil in developing this business. Patil is a low-profile, unassuming agronomist with his feet planted firmly on the ground. In 2014, we were required to de-focus from this initiative which neither Reliance Foundation nor the organized retail initiative of Reliance Industries was interested in. It was too tiny to tickle their senses. But I could not reconcile myself to their disinterest.

I have always been convinced about a potentially large opportunity in upgrading horticulture farm practices in India, developing post-harvest and processing facilities and marketing value-added processed, as well as table-grade horticulture products, to global markets. Patil took the decision in his stride and is now engaged in liaison work with government agencies.

Sadly, most of these professionals who came on board had to migrate to Reliance Industries Limited. This was when a decision was taken in Maker Chambers to get us to focus solely on medical biotechnology. I suppose such a situation is a product of dynamic management.

My pangs of separation following the departure of plant biotechnology, industrial biotechnology, biofuels and agro-based food products from Reliance Life Sciences continued for a period of time. I suppose it is natural for anyone who builds a development-driven business with passion to feel this way. Emotions do exist and must be managed.

SEPARATING ONESELF

These separations also sensitized me to the fact that, at some stage, I myself would have to step away from Reliance Life Sciences, just as booster rockets have to leave a spacecraft after helping it accelerate to leave gravity. It was getting time to initiate the process of 'letting go'. All through its formative years, I had to get involved across the breadth of the organization and delve into its depths. This meant engaging with every one of the management team members and with most other colleagues.

Up to a point in time, I could relate to almost every person in the organization. I could address them by their first names. But beyond the year 2010, this became difficult as more team members came on board. I had to give up the practice of interviewing every single candidate intending to join Reliance Life Sciences. I had to step back from specific pricing decisions. I had to stay away from approving purchase orders, except for those beyond an appropriate value relative to our business size. I also had to stay away from operational decisions, and had to foster the next generation of leaders to potentially take my position.

In 2013, I started thinking about this more deeply. It dawned on me that I had to first change my mindset. The sense of attachment to a business that you have seen since its conception, had to go. There were three segments of the business that had been jettisoned. The first was plant biotechnology, and within it biofuels, to Reliance Foundation. The second was industrial biotechnology to the technology group of Reliance Industries. Both were not my doing though. The third was the closure of the assisted reproduction facility. All three events had taught me to disengage myself beyond a point.

This sense of disengagement was not very difficult to achieve. It helped that I did not get carried away by titles, position, power and status. I am also not the type to get overawed by anyone, even the rich and famous. My upbringing was all about humility and modesty. I was brought up to have confidence in my abilities, to let my work speak for itself; to think before saying something, and to speak with understatement. To this day, when I step into a five-star hotel, I feel embarrassed by its lavishness. At airports, as a 'commercially important passenger', airline staff would invariably have me escorted inside, but I would politely refuse their help on the ground that I was familiar with the airport. If I was not, I could easily find my way around.

My wife, Saroj is in the same mould. She does not drive a car and prefers to use the bus to commute to her school. Only in a time-constrained situation does she take a taxi. Both of us were clear that, after I stepped down from Reliance Life Sciences, we would scale down our material needs and live within our means, based on our savings. The cost of our apartment in Mumbai, as well as the fees for my son's undergraduate and masters' studies, came out of our savings. I had not taken recourse to borrowing money. I am neither driven by corporate position nor status, which to me is a form of hallucination. Titles do not matter to me the way they matter to the external world.

While I planned to step back, I did not completely disengage from Reliance Life Sciences. The disengagement had to happen over time to make it seamless and effective. I have had to be engaged in such a way as to be able to guide and steer Reliance Life Sciences through a crucial phase of scaling up its business organization. Concurrently, I had to provide guidance to the leadership to make the grade. I had to play tough and soft at the same time.

LETTING GO

Reliance Life Sciences was gaining momentum. The innovation engine was seeing products and services being translated into revenue and cash flows. Manufacturing facilities were increasingly getting occupied and capacities being utilized. Sub-cultures were being ingrained. Marketing was getting recognition from customers and gaining in strength.

From the financial year 2014-15, I brought in a new management framework, with the approval of Mukesh Ambani. The objective was to bring about better delegation of powers, along with greater responsibility and accountability for business heads, initiative heads and key functional heads. This was also part of the process of preparing and grooming the next level of leadership to take my place.

It was time to reduce my participation in review meetings and to leave operational matters to business and key functional heads. It was also time to reduce my span of control and focus on a smaller group of management team members. They would be the drivers of businesses and initiatives and represented the next level of leadership and potential CEOs.

This group, which we called the executive management team, comprised of three categories of leaders. In the first category were the four business heads in plasma proteins, biopharmaceuticals, pharmaceuticals and clinical research. In the second category were the two initiative heads in regenerative medicine and molecular medicine. Six heads of key functions—human resources, science, engineering, information technology, finance and legal/intellectual property—formed the third category.

I defined principles for decisions to help improve the quality of decision-making. I instituted a new granular performance management system that was relatively more measurable and which enabled self-evaluation of performance scores. I made it clear that I would focus on new areas. Principles for decision-making centred around business decisions in each domain and function—minimum netback price levels, hiring within the corporate plan provisions, upper value limit for purchase decisions and no compromise on quality. I also insisted on zero tolerance of issues related to integrity, gender discrimination, compliance with good practices, regulatory and tax compliance, health, safety and environment aspects and timely management reporting. Also, that all key decisions were to be documented as per a defined format and signed off by the leadership involved in the decisions. Above all, there was a strong focus on month-to-month cash profits and cash flows.

I also gave the team two criteria which would help them take a decision when faced with a dilemma. 'Ask what is in the interest of the customer and what is in the interest of the organization and you will invariably find the answer.' I encouraged them to be quick and responsive and to appreciate that decisions were made in a context of uncertainty, not necessarily based on perfect information, and the prevailing product-market-industry-economy context. 'You must not regret a decision in hindsight,' I would say.

Thus, with greater delegation of powers, with responsibility and accountability, and constant guidance, Reliance Life Sciences got better at creating potential CEO-quality leaders. This was necessary as the company scaled up, moved into more and more markets and created new corporate business units.

IDENTIFYING SUCCESSORS

Soon it was time to identify and groom successors. I wrote to Mukesh Ambani and talked about my plans to step down in about two years, when I would turn fifty-eight. I mentioned that I wished to do something else. If he required, I could spend a couple of years as a mentor in Reliance Life Sciences, staying away from operational responsibilities. I had identified a few colleagues who could potentially succeed me. In my communication, I wrote that, in case he was planning to consider a lateral hire, he must give an equal and fair opportunity to internal candidates. This was for the sake of continuity of the growth path, and more importantly, to place Reliance Life Sciences on the right trajectory to reach a billion US dollars in revenues.

Mukesh Ambani would have none of this. He wrote back just one line saying that I should work till I was sixty-five years of age. I wrote back explaining why it was important for me and for Reliance Life Sciences to identify and groom successors. He wanted to discuss the matter but the meeting did not take place. It was his way of saying that he did not want to enter into a discussion.

Indirectly it was his way of affirming faith in me. Nevertheless, I had decided to identify successors from within Reliance Life Sciences. I conferred with them and made up my mind to let go of the reins of Reliance Life Sciences. If anything, my efforts would develop the next rung of leaders who could run businesses first and then grow to be CEO.

IMPERFECT FIT

I don't have a biology background and had never built and run a company before Reliance Life Sciences. The closest I had come to this was to identify opportunities, conceptualize the architecture, develop a core team and work with them to get traction. But I was mandated to start a life sciences company.

Before Reliance Life Sciences, in the year 2002, I was called to project manage the promotion for the initial public equity stock offer by IPCL, the first for a public sector company in India. I did not have any experience in this. Similarly, I was asked to project manage due diligence for the acquisition of IPCL by Reliance in the year 2002 when I had never done this before. Much earlier, in 1989, I was asked to take additional responsibility for corporate communications in IPCL by Hasmukh Shah, when I had no prior experience.

There are many such examples, which only go to show that it would do well not to look for a perfect fit with regard to experience and expertise for a role in organizations. This is not only true for CEO positions but for almost all positions in organizations. The exception is with resources who are highly-skilled and/or are statutorily mandated on their education, experience and licence-holding requirements. Instead of looking for the perfect lead, it is better to start with a person who is not fully there, but has the potential, and provide the right environment for this person to learn and develop. Trust and empowerment create motivation. Application of mind by the individual and his/her quiet confidence do the rest.

PREPARING FOR SEPARATION PANGS

It occurred to me that I must document the trials, tribulations and learning in building the life sciences initiative from scratch. This, I thought, would be useful to colleagues in the Reliance group and entrepreneurs in general. Around the time that I was contemplating documenting the life sciences story, Rahul Padhye spoke to me about a friend of his, who had built a social media company from scratch. Rahul's friend wanted me to address his 200-odd employees on the Reliance Life Sciences story. I accepted the invitation. When I spoke, I adopted an open and informal style. This was in contrast to my usual semi-formal style of speaking at conferences, whether as a standalone speaker or as a panelist.

Later that evening, when I returned home, I wrote out the points I had made to the gathering and sent it to Mukesh Ambani. I added a comment that I was contemplating writing a book on my learning. He promptly encouraged me. That was the genesis of this book, which in a sense, is the beginning of the process of letting go.

When you pen down your experiences, the separation pangs get diluted. This also happens when you share your problems with your near and dear ones, which in my case, is often my wife. By writing about my experiences, I believed I could give insights to future managers within Reliance Life Sciences, the Reliance group companies and other companies. I could also help and inspire startups and potential entrepreneurs.

TESTING METTLE

Having a methodology for succession and smooth transition also allowed me a two-year window of opportunity to assess how the next line of leadership would make the grade. This meant an assessment of potential future leaders on several parameters:

- Ability to engage with people, programmes and projects.
- Capability to set high standards of performance, transparency and integrity for oneself.
- Adeptness to drive performance.
- Will to beat expectations.
- Tenacity and resolve to make things succeed.

- Courage to take setbacks in one's stride, and move forward.
- Aptitude to relate to and manage external constituencies.
- Faculty to deal with demands of the chairman and board of directors.

Soon enough, one of the internal leaders came to me saying he was opting out of being considered for the CEO position. He preferred to first be a successful business head. I respected his decision, although he was not very clear about his reasons for coming to this decision.

STRESS-TESTING

Letting go is not an impulsive decision. Thinking about letting go and then making this known to the leadership team, takes some effort. It involves opening up the CEO position for other competent individuals. It entails reconciliation, and above all, an acceptance that the organization can do well, possibly even better, without you. At the same time, it requires systems and processes to be reinforced, and communication to be frequent. It involves protecting potential successors from the naysayers who are out to prove they don't have what it takes.

It then requires a period of hand-holding to ensure that the successor gets on track, followed by a period of stress-testing your colleagues and progressively weaning yourself off the job. One stress-testing technique is to deliberately stay away from a crisis situation to see how the successor performs, and step in, if required, at the right time just before matters come to a stalemate. Another way is to set stretched targets in terms of financial numbers, schedules and costs, and to push back proposed options and ask for an out-of-the-box solution.

Stress testing is important to assess who is capable and who is not. It is required because, in a CEO's world, there is much loneliness. The role, and the responsibility that goes along with it, are demanding—group corporate resources in Maker Chambers have to be managed on one side, and a diverse team across the organization has to be managed on the other side. All this, while driving performance, upholding the cultural aspects of the organization, being its face to the external world and being open, warm and supportive of team members and constituencies. Not everyone makes the grade. Only those who emerge unscathed in the pressure test, and have the right values and norms of behaviour, can be in the reckoning.

BEING DISPASSIONATE

During this letting go process, you must be dispassionate. It is a strange situation and an odd feeling. On the one hand, you cannot be less passionate with the organization; you must have that passion for the organization throughout your lifetime. On the other hand, you must have a sense of being distanced from the organization.

The closest parallel that comes to my mind is the time, in August 2007, when my son was set to leave home to join the undergraduate programme in mechanical engineering at the Georgia Institute of Technology or Georgia Tech, in Atlanta, USA. My wife and I had to get prepared for a home without him. When we were leaving for the airport to see him off for the Jet Airways flight to Newark, I told her not to cry because it would make him feel bad. During the car ride to the airport, she kept quiet. I realized that she was putting up a brave front. I was doing the talking, while driving, to lighten the mood. What happened at the airport surprised, as well as annoyed her. My son took his leave and strode confidently into the airport terminal. We waited to see if he would look back and wave. He did not. Before she could react, I simply told her, 'He has grown up and we have to let go.' We returned home quietly.

BIDDING ADIEU

Since Reliance Life Sciences was becoming an 'adult', I was developing a mindset of letting it go. It's a strange feeling similar to what I had felt, years ago, when my seventeen-year old son was ready to go to the US for his undergraduate studies. Letting go inherently has a huge responsibility; of leaving the organization in a strong state with the ability to grow revenues at high rates, combined with high profitability, in the years to come. Letting go of an organization that is weak and infirm would sound its death knell, unless of course, the CEO is not up to the mark and wants to escape.

I can well imagine that when I come to a stage of bidding adieu, it will not be easy. I have been engaged with the company even before its birth, and have nurtured it, hand-picked its leadership team members, worked shoulder to shoulder with them, and watched it grow. Until I leave, my efforts will be focused on strengthening the foundation of the organization and nurturing its structures for development, growth, profitability and sustenance.

RENUNCIATION

My portrayal of letting go of Reliance Life Sciences may seem self-laudatory. This is not the case. My only intention is to give insights into my personal context and thinking, to give future leaders a sense of preparing to let go of their creations when the time comes.

FOUNDATION FORGOTTEN, SUPERSTRUCTURE SEEN

When we see large and successful organizations, we only see the superstructure. We do not think of the foundation. When we see skyscrapers or a large heritage building, we are in awe of the super structure. We rarely think about those who slogged to build the foundation: Digging up dirt, doing the arduous rock-blasting on site, piling for columns, battling with ground water seepage, getting building permits and regulatory approvals, engaging with construction safety, getting construction integrity with design, procuring within cost and time, validating, qualifying facilities, and commercializing. The builders did all this only to step back and hand over the building to the new owners and tenants, so that they could give it life and character.

After my experience at Reliance Life Sciences, I have started to see an ancient place of worship, a heritage building, a large manufacturing facility, a magnificent product or an organization, in a different way. There are many examples of imposing structures, such as Lutyen's Delhi, Vidhan Soudha in Bengaluru, Panama Canal, Airbus 380, BASF manufacturing site in Germany, Indian Railways, Indian Oil Corporation and Taj Mahal, to name a few. And, of course, the Jamnagar site of Reliance Industries Limited. In all these cases, I think about the mind of the architect who could conceive of something so expansive, monumental and intricate. I reflect on the person's and team's ability, not only to envision but to give the vision shape, form and character, making it work, and at the end of it all, letting it go.

PART B

Experiential Learning

10

PAUSING TO REFLECT AND LEARN

'Metaphors demystify concepts and
make learning fun.'

Reflecting on experiences is undoubtedly rewarding. It provides a treasure-trove of learning. Ruminating on occurrences and correlating them with parallels help decipher perceptions, simplify them and make others' understanding that much easier. If the parallel is amusing, then there is a fun element to it.

Historical understandings can be varied—some serious, some entertaining and some plain bizarre. It's not easy to draw a common theme across them. At best, they can be a collage of experiential constructs.

But there are limitations to using experiential constructs in drawing analogies. For example, using past experiences to draw a parallel to a context, a group of people or an individual, can be counterproductive in the absence of sensitivity to the situation where this is used. Whether in a family situation or in an organization setting, they can turn out to be irrelevant.

MEDLEY OF ANALOGIES

I have often pondered over the experiences and learning that my colleagues and I have had during the building of Reliance Life Sciences. No doubt I have been a rank outsider in the biotechnology industry, as have many of my colleagues. But the saving grace is that I have had exposure to several business sectors, functional disciplines, education fields, languages, cultures and geographies during my career, which has helped me adapt to this new industry. I tried to make biotechnology simple so that I could understand it better. This led me to draw analogies—the parallels that I saw—between biotechnology and some of the domains that I could relate to. Analogies help simplify learning. They help to add some humour to the situation as well.

At times, I would use a parallel from society, and its myriad practices and beliefs. I shared these analogies with my colleagues in a light-hearted manner, with no malice towards anyone. This helped me understand issues better. It also helped put these issues in perspective. However, these analogies made some of my colleagues squirm and some others seethe with anger. But, most of them were amused. I could tell this from the expressions on their faces.

MUMBO JUMBO

To the uninitiated, biotechnology represents mumbo jumbo. My experience has been that, even for many biotechnologists, it is mumbo jumbo. This is primarily because of the ignorance of such biotechnologists. I am not being negative in saying this. Ignorance partly arises from the mammoth unexplored frontiers of its expanse, and partly, in their limited ability to ask the stupidest of questions. I neither had such baggage of biology nor was I worried about asking stupid questions. I wanted to learn, and I have the same mindset to this day. I tend to ask a lot of fundamental questions.

I remember asking my seventh grade science teacher in school why it is that when you go higher in altitude, it gets colder. On the contrary, it should get hotter as you are getting closer to the sun. She was upset with me and ordered me to sit down. Later, I figured out the answer myself.

One of the action learning principles propounded by Dr Reg Revans is, 'Questioning is essential to gaining new insights.' I do raise questions—fearless ones at that. For I have neither baggage from the past nor fear of the unknown. Questioning has helped me gain insights. I, therefore, encourage colleagues to ask questions. I tell them not to feel embarrassed about asking stupid questions, even if someone laughs at the question.

MONKEYS ON YOUR SHOULDER

Dr Vishwas Sarangdhar once told me a parable that I can never forget—In India, you occasionally come across people who train monkeys to do an act or two, to make a living. Their monkeys sit on their shoulders as the handlers move from village to village. They have to take care of their monkeys. No one else will do it for them.

There's something to learn from this parable. All of us have monkeys on our shoulders—an alternative expression for responsibilities on our shoulders. Each one of us has to take care of the monkeys that sit on our shoulders. Some people are adept at shifting the monkeys from their own shoulders on to your shoulders. If you are not careful enough, soon you will have many monkeys on your shoulders. One or two monkeys may even perch on your head. Therefore, it's best that you ask others to take care of their own monkeys, while you worry about yours.

In organizational terms, work that is to be done by one person is foisted on to others. If you do not push back, you get overburdened, to the extent that you cannot deliver on what you are responsible and accountable for. We have had several such situations in Reliance Life Sciences. Clinical research would want the medical affairs in marketing group to take responsibility for pharmaco-vigilance on the grounds that the product was in the market. Medical affairs would want clinical research to take this responsibility, given that they had better expertise. Whose monkey is pharmaco-vigilance? After much debate we decided that medical affairs would take the responsibility, conforming to the systems and process standards of clinical research.

Another example is laundry. Managing a biotechnology organization demands managing the laundry function. Clean room garments need to be laundered to certain standards and are subject to regulatory audit. Manufacturing would try and shift the responsibility for laundry to the administration on the grounds that it is an administrative responsibility. The favour would be returned with the reasoning that manufacturing is better placed to ensure compliance with good manufacturing practices and regulatory audit. Whose monkey is the laundry function? Again, after some debate, the responsibility was taken by manufacturing for garments used by them with a different colour code.

CARPET BOMBING

In the early days of Reliance Life Sciences, I was intrigued by fertility specialists claiming that they had hundred per cent success rates in in-vitro fertility treatments. I could not believe them. Such claims sounded like sales pitches. These fertility specialists catered to patients who could afford the high-cost fertility treatments, cycle after cycle.

Soon, after questioning, it became clear to me that they resort to 'carpet bombing', a bombing strategy in traditional wars. In biological terms, this begins with hyper-stimulation to have a female produce several eggs. They then fertilize the eggs in-vitro and push many fertilized eggs back into the uterus. After this, they carry out a careful selection of highly viable fertilized eggs and destroy the others. No wonder they have a hundred per cent success rate!

DUEL OF THE DUAL

Sanskrit is one language which provides for the dual of a noun. Very similar to the matrix in mathematics, one, two and many form the columns, and prepositions form the rows. In many fields of industry, economics, academia and politics, you see this playing out. Unlike Sanskrit, in most of these situations, if not all, there is a duel between the dual—two schools of thought constantly bickering and fighting with each other for supremacy. It leads to damage. This is so because each school of thought or school of science or proponent of a technology, thinks that their school or proposition is the best. They rarely consider peaceful co-existence as an option, and try to undermine each other all the time.

From my engagement with corporate business development in several spheres, I found that the duel between the dual exists in many domains:

- Crystalline vs thin-film photovoltaic cells in solar energy.
- Technical vs fundamental analysts in stock markets.
- Boeing vs Airbus in aviation.
- GSM vs CDMA in mobile phone technology.
- Rightists and leftists, Labour vs Conservatives and Republicans vs Democrats in politics.
- Catholics vs Protestants, Shias vs Sunnis and Vaishnavites vs Shaivaites in religion.

The conflict for supremacy causes unnecessary friction.

Initially in Reliance Life Sciences, we had two lobbies among stem cell biologists—embryonic and adult stem cell sciences. Each lobby believed that their approach was the best and a panacea for all problems. Often, they would have academic debates in which they would be rude to each other, aggressively propagating their belief to the detriment of science. In such situations, the organization's objectives became secondary to the individual scientist's beliefs. There was a tendency to impose individual perspectives which often resulted in science projects suffering from lack of progress and not moving forward into the development stage. Above all, there was a waste of energy and low flash points.

In such situations, it is best not to get swayed by either school of thought. It helps to make a dispassionate and critical assessment of both sides from several angles—customer-friendliness, technological challenges and evolution, cost-competitiveness and societal adaptation, among others.

TIRUPATI BARBER

There is an old saying that you should not do your work like that of a Tirupati barber. This means leaving a task half done and getting on to something else. My parents had explained this age-old concept to us during our childhood days. I find it prevalent in many organizations.

Tirupati is among the topmost pilgrimage places for Hindus in India. It is the abode of a temple to Lord Venkateswara, or Balaji, as the deity is known in north India, an incarnation of Lord Vishnu. It is said that in the good old days, the barbers in Tirupati were a law unto themselves. Millions of pilgrims would come to Tirupati. Many of them would tonsure their heads to donate their hair to the presiding deity. The Tirupati barber would tonsure one part of the head of a customer. Then, he would go away to seek another customer. The poor first customer had to wait till the barber returned. He or she could not walk away. No other barber would touch a half-tonsured head and complete the job.

On a good day, each barber would have a few anxious,

and often angry customers. These customers would be at their wits' end with their 'hair-razing' experience. But their protests had no impact on the barbers. The next time around too, the barbers would treat them the same way. The customers had no choice.

All this changed once the government of the erstwhile Andhra Pradesh state, where Tirupati is located, took over the temple administration. Order was brought about. Designated places for tonsure were created. A system of standard rates and tokens for sequencing were introduced and one tonsure job had to be completed before the next client could be taken up.

You regularly encounter Tirupati barbers in organizations, individuals who leave a job half done only to get on with another task or assignment. In Reliance Life Sciences, I have seen such behaviour with some colleagues working on one problem, struggling with it and losing interest, and then getting on with a new problem. In the process, a lot of money and time is lost. When I see potential Tirupati barbers in Reliance Life Sciences, I caution them. I bluntly tell them to get the work on hand completed first before worrying about another task.

Some scientists also fall in this category. They have no concern for wasted resources, including the valuable resource that time represents, when a project is shelved. By the time the project is given up, the company would have spent money filing provisional patents, a paper or two would have been written, and a patent or two with no commercial value would have been filed, only to be eventually written off. Sooner or later, the scientists involved would quit only to repeat the process all over again, in the same or an allied field, in other organizations.

NOMADIC SLAVES

Reliance Life Sciences has hired several scientists of Indian origin who have worked in the US or the UK. With some rare exceptions though, they belong to a tribe called 'post-docs', in simple terms, nomadic slaves. They join a university or institute of repute as a post-doctoral scholar working under a federal grant-funded project of a senior tenured professor there. The appointment is typically for three years. Sometimes spouses work in the same university. Once the term gets over, they continue if the faculty member can get an extension, with or without grants on the project, or assign them to another project. Otherwise, they pack their bags and move to another university.

These post-docs work long hours in cramped research laboratories and are enslaved to the faculty. They have no place to call their own. They live the dreams of others. The higher the ranking of a university, the lower the pay of a post-doc. I know of post-docs in reputed universities who are paid less than what a secretary in a company earns in the US. Bright talent goes for a song. Once they get tired or when family situations demand, they go back.

I have found that scientists who join us from commercial organizations are relatively better committed to costs, time schedules and to the long-term interests of the organization. Though this has been my experience, I would not like to undermine researchers from an academic background.

MIGRATORY WINTER BIRDS

Then, we have the migratory winter birds, overseas Indians who come to India during December and January. They ask for meetings to explore research collaboration and organizational partnerships. Some want to explore relocation for employment. Some of them link their requests for meetings to visits with their family for social purposes. Invariably, these visits do not result in much traction.

The more enterprising of these overseas visitors want perks such as a car to pick them up and drop them. Some of them even want free transport arrangements to places of pilgrimage, or places of tourist interest near Mumbai. Initially we would get taken in by these people and prepare ourselves well, but soon it dawned on us that we were being exploited for personal gain.

MOTHERS-IN-LAW

The traditional perception of a mother-in-law in India is of someone who personifies a bossy, demanding and loud individual, always finding fault with the daughter-in-law. In organizations, we see mothers-in-law too. They are team members, female and male alike. They don't do much work. They just sit on a wall and demand that others work. They try to get work done without lifting a finger. They boss, fret and fume, breathe down your neck. They are in a constant blame game.

At Reliance Life Sciences, I have seen 'mothers-in-law' in business, manufacturing, finance and research while 'daughters-in-law' are typically in marketing, support services such as human resources and administration. These are thankless functions. When things are going fine, they are forgotten. People remember them only when something has not happened. The delineation is not cast in stone, though. It varies with how strong or weak the business head or support service head is.

When I see such behaviour, I stop the concerned person and say, 'Please don't behave like the archetypal mother-in-law. Get going yourself and get the job done.' This is an exaggerated view, naturally. But, nevertheless, it tells one about whom in the organization to watch out for, and take corrective action against.

GOAT ENTERING A BUTCHER'S SHOP

Have you ever felt like a goat entering a butcher's shop? If not, wait till you get into a meeting with a regulatory auditor, an irate customer, a vendor with overdue payments, or a meeting at a government official's chambers or an in-person or video conference performance review. I have to admit that I feel like the not-so-proverbial sacrificial goat in these situations. Fortunately or unfortunately for the goat, it never realizes what it is in for, unlike human beings who have to go through the experience knowing exactly what to expect!

CASTOR OIL

Review meetings are no fun; not for me and not for my colleagues either, I am sure. But these meetings can be 'fun' in a different way if you become an observer and pay attention to the body language of the participants and the mood in the room. I am often amused by colleagues who look so sour, as if they had consumed castor oil the night before to relieve themselves from constipation. In my younger days, when there were limited options to deal with constipation, castor oil was an effective remedy. You had to gulp down the bitter potion and wait expectantly for relief the next morning.

I suppose many colleagues feel like this due to the rigour of review meetings. The relief visible on the faces of the participants when I proclaim that the meeting will be closed in ten minutes has to be seen to be believed. On the other hand, when the meeting is extended beyond the scheduled time, the despair in the room is palpable.

Review meetings are a necessary evil to drive performance, and have to be endured with a 'grin and bear it' attitude. I don't believe that employees and organizations are so evolved that things happen without a managing framework. To me, that is a utopian concept. If Reliance Life Sciences has come this far, regular review meetings, as part of a defined managing framework, have been, arguably, an important contributor, whether we like it or not. In this case, castor oil is unlikely to help relieve the discomfort!

WASHERMAN'S DONKEYS

A former colleague, the late A.P. Singh, was a witty person with a down-to-earth sense of humour who would talk of organizations having employees who are like the proverbial washerman's donkeys in north India. Sadly, he is no longer with us. These donkeys neither belong to the house nor to the river bank where clothes are washed in many villages. The donkey's job is to transport the wash load from the laundry man's house to the river bank and back. When they are not on transport duty, the donkeys just hang around, not knowing where to go or what to do.

Organizations also have such donkeys. Pardon me for this analogy, no offence meant to anyone. Typically, these are very senior executives who are paid highly for the fear of losing them to competitors, but they have little work. They do not leave the company, having become used to the comforts and perks without much work. Fortunately we don't have washerman's donkeys in Reliance Life Sciences. We can neither afford them nor will our hands-on culture permit them. They are likely to be found in rich organizations that are fearful of competition.

PANJARA POLE

Panjara pole is a term used by my good friend and a former colleague, Devendra Amin, who lives in Vadodara in Gujarat state. It is an extension of the washerman's donkey analogy. In the state of Gujarat, there are designated 'panjara poles' or old age homes for cattle, that societies maintain. The cattle are fed and taken care of till they die. Cattle are not sent to the abattoir. Many Hindus are vegetarians and those who do eat meat usually do not eat beef; hence, the concept of panjara poles maintained by social organizations as not-for-profit entities. These are places where the cattle are taken care of, for past services rendered, as well as out of a tradition of respecting animals that serve mankind.

Organizations have 'panjara poles', which are parking lots for the older employees in the organization in consideration for past services rendered. As with washerman's donkeys, these employees are retained out of concern that they could be of better value to competitors, or they could reveal the skeletons in the organization's closet, if they left. These employees continue to enjoy their pay and perks well into old age, even after they are too old to work. They just 'chew the cud' and occasionally make their presence felt. Again, pardon me for using an animate analogy. No offence meant.

At Reliance Life Sciences, we don't provide panjara poles. We cannot afford such parking lots and even if we could afford them, we would not have them, as it is against the policy of the company which believes in making way for the younger generation and creating opportunities for them. At Reliance Life Sciences, we believe in constantly working on new thoughts and ideas. Opportunities for younger team members must be found, through the growth of the organization, both in quantitative and qualitative terms.

The unwritten practice at Reliance Life Sciences is for a team member to get an extension of two years after the formal retirement age of fifty-eight. This is an option if the person has been with the company for a long time, is required for his/her skill sets and expresses a desire to continue. In some exceptional cases, a further extension till the age of sixty-five is granted. This norm was established by Founder Chairman Dhirubhai Ambani, who wanted good people to work as long as they could physically work and add value to the organization.

PARROTS

The term 'parrot' also is used from my former colleague Devendra Amin. Every organization has its parrots who tend to be 'yes men', agreeing with whatever they are told. You can also see these people on the streets—smartly dressed salesmen who are trained to say the same thing from morning till evening. 'Two units of X brand of pain balm and one pencil free,' was Devendra Amin's favourite example of their dialogue.

In north Indian villages, one person wishes the other by invoking the name of God saying 'Ram, Ram'. If a parrot was present, it would repeat the words 'Ram, Ram' if anyone or anything passed by, even if a cricket ball thrown by a child playing cricket on the street, passed by.

In organizations, parrots represent the tribe of yes men and women, who would say, 'Yes Sir!' or 'Yes Madam!' for every statement emanating from their bosses. Such people are dangerous. Imagine the whole organization saying 'Ram, Ram'. You can't expect much success in such an organization.

In Reliance Life Sciences, I did not encourage 'yes men'. Every person, irrespective of hierarchy was welcome to disagree with my views, but this must be followed by constructive suggestions or solutions. The more innovative and entrepreneurial an organization is, the greater the latitude colleagues have to express their views, thoughts and suggestions. In my experience, it is typically the unsure, shaky, fearful or underperforming employees who become 'yes men'. Sometimes, those who have skeletons in the cupboard become 'yes men'. If you find someone saying yes too often, then you know you have a situation to deal with.

LORD LONDON

The term 'Lord London' comes from the period of British rule in India. 'Lord London' refers to a member of the British parliament, typically a member of the upper house, who would discuss matters of national interest and legislate. Organizations have their share of Lord Londons. The plural of the city's name is intentional, to indicate Indian English. Lord Londons are those who sit around, warming their seats and bossing around, telling others what to do. They do not want to wet their hands, let alone get their hands dirty.

Lord Londons soon earn the disdain of others. But they thrive in some organizations. They are the 'gin and tonic' networking types, know how to hold their glass, can tell the difference between a Chardonnay and a Sauvignon, drop names liberally and love to narrate stories from the past, whether listeners want to hear them or not. Somehow, they do manage to get a small audience and have an uncanny ability to be at the right place at the right time, and are perceived to be doing the right things.

You do not find them in Reliance, more so in Reliance Life Sciences where parties are only held to celebrate a year of hard work, such as the annual April party, or for a key achievement. We are merciless with Lord Londons.

AIRPORT SECURITY

In 2014, we commissioned our oncology injectable manufacturing facility, 'Plant 6', as we called it. Plant 6 was based on state-of-the-art isolator technology. Simply put, the filling, bunging, lyophilization and sealing sections of the filling line were enclosed in a negative relative pressure chamber. This was designed to keep the carcinogenic drug formulations, which are cytotoxic, within the enclosure, so that they would not leak outside. The tunnel of the vial heating section had a high efficiency particulate matter filter that permitted air into the area with only very few particles in it. The filter was failing in integrity tests because of gaps between its outer surfaces and the tunnel. At the same time, it was determined that, post-filtration, the number of particles was within limits.

In this situation, the dilemma was whether to move on with the filling of exhibit batches or to wait for the filter integrity to be confirmed. There were two schools of thought—one claimed there were no particles downstream and it was fine to go ahead. The other school was of the opinion that the commissioning should be done in sequence.

With no resolution in sight, the differing views were escalated to me. I gave them a simple analogy: the filter was analogous to airport security. There could be integrity issues with the security screening. But even if hijackers were not detected during the security screening, it did not mean that everything was fine. I said that the filter integrity had to be established first and the particle count had to be within limits. Only after that could the filling of exhibit batches be taken up.

MEANINGLESS MARRIAGES

In 2014, the process of closing several out-licensing deals for biosimilars was long and arduous. Almost every negotiation would stretch for many months and either culminate in a deal or would end up as a damp squib, without any result. This process would often be very frustrating. It involved a lot of international travel through several time zones, very often back-to-back travel, moving across very different weather situations. On one occasion, we moved from +30 ^{0}C to -30 ^{0}C when we travelled from Mumbai to Moscow in the first week of February 2012. It happened to be the coldest day in Moscow. Rahul Padhye and I patiently told ourselves that we would not sacrifice long-term interest for the sake of short-term cash flows and profitability.

However challenging and frustrating these processes were, they did have their share of lighter moments. During one particular negotiation, the potential out-licensing partner wanted to keep the option of buying the same biopharmaceutical product from another company, or wanted us to match the lower price. His contention was that if a better offer came along during the agreement period, their company should have the freedom to take it. In the same breath, the company wanted an exclusive deal. After they mentioned this, there was a short period of studied silence in the room.

I found the whole demand ridiculous. It was the first time ever that a company had come up with such a demand. I replied in a diplomatic manner by giving an analogy. I told the other company team that this demand was like a meaningless marriage proposition. I asked them to imagine that they were going into wedlock and wanted the partner to agree to a condition that, after the marriage and any time till they died, the partner must agree to a separation if a younger and/or a more beautiful or handsome person came along and proposed to the partner. Alternatively, the partner must match the age and looks of the new person. For a moment, the out-licensing company did not know what had hit them. They quickly realized how ridiculous their demand was and did not press any further. We closed the out-licensing deal that night, after day long negotiations.

COCKROACH'S MOUSTACHE

B.C. Rai, my former boss in IPCL, would tell us youngsters to watch out for the cockroach's moustache. In saying this, he was referring to the whiskers of the cockroach. He would say that first the whisker would come through a crack. And soon enough, the full cockroach would come into the room. He used to use this analogy for those people who negotiated or used resources. First, there would be a very small request for a point of view or term of agreement to be incorporated. Sometimes, this would be in the form of a request to use a financial, material or infrastructural facility. Being small and not of much consequence, you would accede to the request. Soon enough, these minor requests would balloon into major ones and before you realized it, you would have allowed another party to set up camp in your backyard.

This analogy has stood me in good stead in negotiations and in permitting resource use or in dealing with non-compliance.

Some persons or companies tend to ask for accommodation of one clause. You give in gracefully because it does not matter much materially. Then after a while another request is made. This continues till you have given away a lot. I found it sensible to first understand positions across all key terms or clauses before converging. Otherwise, you may find that the ground has moved beneath your feet.

TAJ MAHAL

All of us know that the Taj Mahal in Agra is a masterpiece of architecture. It is a timeless monument of love. We have 'Taj Mahals' in science as well, which are expensive pieces of equipment that are bought for the love of science, hardly used, and become relics. In the early years of Reliance Life Sciences, I came across two such 'Taj Mahals'. A national research laboratory in India had spent a fortune on a chemical synthesizer. It was hardly used and became a showpiece to impress visitors.

In the second instance, a start-up company in the Silicon Valley had bought a high-throughput screening machine with hardly any workload. It took months for the company to come up with diverse molecular structures and samples so the machine, which could screen 300,000 samples in a relatively short time, was mostly idle. The national laboratory continues to survive on funding by public money. But the Silicon Valley start-up went down the tube with its high cash burn. These are examples of pieces of equipment that are grand, but have become monuments.

At Reliance Life Sciences, we bought one such 'Taj Mahal' in the form of a microarray system. The head of the research group had made ardent appeals that we should have a microarray system and we eventually gave in and bought it. It cost us a bomb. Soon enough, the group head, who was past retirement age, left the organization, after having a few papers published. The expenses piled up when, the software for the microarray system needed to be upgraded at a huge price. Eventually, the equipment vendor, who was in a monopolistic position, stopped servicing the machine. We were stuck with a 'Taj Mahal'.

I was very disappointed with this sequence of events. The money spent for that capital asset could have been used for other purposes. I would joke that, at least, the Taj Mahal earns money with tourists coming from all over the world to see it. In addition, it contributes a lot to the local economy and employment.

I would then chide colleagues who had a long wish list of equipment for purchase that, like the Taj Mahal, we should have a monument for the love of science in the atrium of the life sciences campus. The monument would be the microarray system, duly restored as a relic, a centerpiece and a reminder not to go overboard on spending on resources. This experience taught me, rather painfully, to be extra careful and conservative about expenditure on equipment purchases, facility dimensioning and office spaces. Subsequently, we would ensure that instead of buying new equipment, we would outsource the test or experiment, hire the equipment or even borrow it, if possible. The underlying principle was that there can be no compromise with science, but one needs to be prudent.

COW AND CALF

The other aspect that one has to be careful about in purchases, is the cow and calf syndrome. This essentially refers to an adjunct piece of equipment, consumables, software or interface systems that account for additional costs and blunt the cost effectiveness of a product. With the microarray system, the chips were expensive since they had to be tailor-made, making the calf heavier than the cow.

I once got a Sony Viao low-weight company laptop. It

weighed just 700 gms. The objective was to help me travel light after my unfortunate head injury in March 2013. The weight advantage was lost because the power cable, USB cable and the audio-video adaptor weighed much more.

CARROM BOARD

A former colleague taught me this about organizational dynamics. In a carrom board game, uninitiated spectators are watching which coin the carrom hits, and if it falls into the pocket. You have to be careful, he would say. Don't wait to see which coin the carrom hits, and whether it falls into the pocket or not. See which other coins are hit, where those coins end up on the board and which ones fall into the pocket.

This is true for organizations. Any change should not be seen in isolation, but in a larger relative positional context. A competitor's move must be seen in its entirety. A transfer order must be seen in terms of the impact on relative positions. An explicit statement must be seen for its hidden messages. There are several other diverse applications for this analogy.

11

DEALING WITH CHALLENGES

'Building a business is about breaking
one barrier after another.'

*Opportunities and challenges are like conjoined twins. They
go hand in hand and are fused together, and present a
formidable frontier to engage in and explore. Challenges are
demanding and last a long time. Opportunities, on the other
hand, are relatively less demanding and fleeting. Both of them
require quick intervention, sustained focus and intensity of
engagement to win. However, the most important test is how
a new, resource-constrained organization faces one challenge
after another, in a never-ending stream, and overcomes them.*

COPIOUS CHALLENGES

Reliance Life Sciences, as one would expect, faced plenty of
daunting challenges. The first set of challenges was typical
for a new company with limited experience and constrained
resources. The second set was unique to the biotechnology
industry constellation. The third set was peculiar to the specific
coordinates of Reliance Life Sciences, operating within a large
and successful conglomerate in an alien arena.

To illustrate, Reliance Life Sciences could not leverage financial resources to acquire or invest quickly in enhancements that many regulatory audits would recommend. It could not spend extra on product promotion in response to competition, or stock more in situations that required it to do so. It could not have depth of resources to factor attrition. Reliance Life Sciences had to encourage multi-skilling. We faced the same situations that many small- and medium- scale companies face. On the brighter side though, these constraints helped us focus on tighter working capital management, productivity and value for money.

INTERNAL MORE THAN EXTERNAL

It is not an overstatement that Reliance Life Sciences has faced more internal challenges than external ones. Part of the problem is size: working in an ultra-large organization such as Reliance Industries. The parent company was about scale and competitiveness, given its participation in businesses in the energy and materials value chain, as well as in customer-facing businesses.

Another challenge has come from some of the senior leaders of the Reliance group. They function as conscience keepers, whether specifically empowered by corporate management or not, but have been alien to the people-, technology- and development-oriented organization that Reliance Life Sciences embodies.

These self-proclaimed conscience keepers from the Reliance group also have a habit of imposing systems and processes on a small company like Reliance Life Sciences. These systems are mostly relevant to a large commodity-business organization that is operating with known business models. In addition, there is often a strong urge to command, control and constrict. Mukesh Ambani's trust and support ensured that all these forces were kept at bay.

The imposition covered advance payments, capital procurement and work order placement, direct and indirect taxes, foreign exchange transactions, accounts payables, receivables, and so on. In contrast, where Reliance shared services had to deliver to vendors of Reliance Life Sciences, the same standards were overlooked. For instance, while Reliance shared services wanted 'C' forms for sales tax from customers in good time, it would not be forthcoming in giving out 'C' forms that it owed to vendors in good time. Delayed payments to common vendors caused by the bureaucracy of the large Reliance group, would result in vendors holding our shipments, despite having no issue with our payment track record.

Internal challenges manifested in many other ways, such as an expectation to see revenues from a transactional model of business without an understanding of the developmental model of business that Reliance Life Sciences characterized. This resulted in mild pontification, periodic pushbacks, and lack of response to resource requirements by those who were alien to the needs of a development-driven organisation. Patience and quiet resolve would win at the end of the day. We had to combine patience with resolve to perform in overcoming these challenges.

In aspects of compliances, by and large, there were no issues except that Reliance Life Sciences came lower in the order of priorities. In other areas, especially shared services, there was a mechanistic approach of having one back office person do one component of the process with a push back. There was often no internal customer service process and no reporting even on leisurely metrics. Often, there were cases of missing documents and no acknowledgements of documents directly submitted.

Not that everything was wrong with internal constrictions. We welcomed internal checks and balances in the productive and purposeful use of resources, conformity to systems and processes and compliance with legal and regulatory requirements. We addressed internal challenges by consistently and persistently articulating the specific character of Reliance Life Sciences, that is, its scientific-technological and product-market character. However, such efforts took away management time and effort that could have otherwise been spent productively.

ONE-SIZE-FITS-ALL

Another challenge was that we were on the fringe of the large and well-to-do Reliance group conglomerate which adopted a 'one-size-fits-all' framework, with certain policies on human resources, travel and entertainment applicable to all companies in the group. There was little regard for the specific industry, business and evolutionary context of Reliance Life Sciences.

The implicit impact of this policy was higher costs for us. Our complaints found no listeners within the system. We had to devise innovative approaches to both conform and adapt them to our context. In this, we would walk the thin edge between conformance to group policies and ensuring the interests of Reliance Life Sciences.

A clear example of this was a strange, unilateral decision taken in October 2014 by a new corporate human resources team in the Reliance group. One fine day, a decision was made to clear reimbursement claims without a review by an employee's superior or group head. We protested against the unilateral nature of the decision and raised a red flag that the change in process of doing away with supervisory review would impose higher and uncontrolled costs on Reliance Life Sciences. As an evolving small company, we could not digest a potentially runaway rise in costs.

But my views were ignored. I was told that Reliance Life Sciences must learn to promote a culture of self-control. To my mind, self-control comes when an enabling culture is fostered and there is a high price to be paid for violations. For example, when the law is imposed quickly and fairly for misdemeanours and perjury, there is conformance whether a citizen is policed or not. Other factors here are the state of evolution of the society, the nature of the issues its people face, and their value systems.

In February 2015, it came to light that a rogue new employee in Reliance Life Sciences had raised a series of false claims on joining expenses that added up to a significant amount. Interestingly, no one was aware of this misdemeanour because the system, by default, would clear reimbursements. The false claims came to light when one large claim was flagged by the system to the superior, setting off an investigation which unearthed the magnitude of the fraud. This time, I was emphatic that we had to revert to our earlier system of operation. I did not mind being labelled as an 'old-world man'. Thankfully, the changes we wanted were incorporated; so much for the 'one-size-fits-all' approach and sensitivity to the unique needs of each business.

I had been a student of change management in business school and knew that changes cannot be brought about unilaterally, except in very critical and emergency-like situations or if the management or governance style is autocratic. Change requires an enabling environment. People who are at the centre of change have to understand and value the change. A very meticulous process has to be followed to enable change, with regular and effective communication being key to it.

SEARCHING AND ENGAGING

Accessing talent for a variety of initiative-based needs has been the greatest challenge for Reliance Life Sciences from the beginning, and continues to this day. It has been particularly difficult in stem cell biology and bio-analytical services, given the limited pool of talent available in these domains. Talent in areas such as biopharmaceutical process development is expensive. High attrition is another issue in this domain, as it is with clinical research services and marketing, particularly at the leadership level. This is not to say that talent is easy to come by, and at competitive costs, in other domains. Interacting with individuals in other technology- and talent-driven organizations showed us that the same challenge confronts these organizations too.

Reliance Life Sciences addressed this issue by institutionalizing the competency development and personal engagement of the core leadership, by the traditional approach of searching for and motivating talented professionals to join. We encouraged one-to-one engagement by leaders with their respective team members. On my part, I made it a point to invest in one-to-one engagement with several colleagues. Our efforts to constantly create opportunities for growth and development did help, which is one reason why Reliance Life Sciences has had very little attrition among its leadership. This has played a very important role in its ability to persistently engage across several innovation domains.

I took it upon myself to focus on soft skills training and development through two-hour programmes at the monthly life sciences retreats, and specific year-long, full-day soft skills sessions and workshops for all team members. I would, and continue to, religiously send a soft copy of the presentations from these sessions to Mukesh Ambani. He, in turn, has them included in the Reliance-wide knowledge management portal. So far, we have had close to one hundred such programmes.

NURTURING WITHIN

Our approach to an institutionalized competency development effort to address the talent challenge took the form of a not-for-profit organization called Reliance Institute of Life Sciences. It was started in the year 2008, very early in our evolution. This organization focused on developing entry-level talent through one-year long young professionals' programmes and, later, through one-year advanced diploma programmes in several domains. In addition, the institute took up competency development in soft skills, domain-specific skills and proficiency programmes. This approach was supplemented to a limited extent, by our own search efforts across the globe for lateral hires.

Creating an institutionalized response to the talent challenge was important. This gave competency development firepower through programme quality, focus on programme roll-out, functionality in pedagogy and above all, academic freedom. In addition, it gave latitude for external academic partnerships, such as those with Mumbai University and Deakin University, that were forged in the years 2003 and 2012 respectively.

In hindsight, this has been, undeniably, the best decision taken by us. My experience with Indian Petrochemicals Corporation Limited and my engagement with the academic side of the Dhirubhai Ambani Institute for Information and Communications Technology or DAIICT, at Gandhinagar in Gujarat, gave me the conviction to adopt this model.

A very senior Indian government official once dismissed Reliance Institute of Life Sciences' efforts in competency development as an effort made in self-interest. He made this remark when I told him about the institute during a Delhi strategy session of the US-India Biopharma Summit, of which I was an advisory council member. I was aghast at the casual and caustic remark, but comforted myself with the thought that such souls have limited perspectives in this context.

What I could not reconcile to was the fact that the statement came from a person at the helm of affairs of a government department. Interestingly, pure government departmental efforts in competency development have not made a mark outside the country's premier educational institutions which, in any case, function as independent entities under the Acts of Parliament. Most large private sector companies in the pharmaceutical and other sectors thought of competency development only when they were decades old. Then they went to town announcing the setting up of such institutes, forgetting that the public sector enterprises in India have been at the forefront of competency development in technical and managerial areas for a long time.

Institutionalizing competency development has been a characteristic of the larger public sector companies and quasi-government bodies. In this regard, organizations such as the State Bank of India, Indian Petrochemicals Corporation Limited, National Thermal Power Corporation Limited, Bhabha Atomic Energy Research Centre, Bharat Heavy Electricals Limited, Steel Authority of India Limited and Life Insurance Corporation of India come to mind. In the private sector, examples include the business house of Tatas, Housing Development Corporation Limited, now HDFC Bank, and ICICI Bank.

GRASS IS MOST OFTEN NOT GREENER ON THE OTHER SIDE

Quite a few of our employees at middle management level left us in the early years, to join other biotechnology and pharmaceutical companies in India and in Southeast Asian countries such as Singapore and Malaysia. Some of them would later write to me that they wanted to come back. They would tell me what a great company Reliance Life Sciences had been for them. Eulogy does not excite us.

There were several peculiar situations in this regard. In one case, a senior manufacturing head left to join a biotechnology company only to see his pay cut by 30 per cent within a month of joining. The company he joined was struggling to pay its employees. Another of our employees joined a multinational company only to want to come back after a week, while a third employee wanted to come back after two years, saying she had left for personal reasons, while her exit interview form said that she was leaving for better prospects. In one instance, a middle management quality control professional said that his mother in Bangalore had cancer and that he wanted to be close to her; later, he joined a Hyderabad-based vaccine company.

Initially, such exits left gaps. But, with the young professional programmes and advanced diploma programmes getting into gear, we were able to address this issue. Once Reliance Life Sciences improved its performance, the issue of regular exits faded into the background. We also formulated a policy making re-hiring an exception.

PULLING THE PLUG

Reliance Life Sciences has faced, and continues to face, a challenge as to when to pull the plug on a research project or a development programme, or when it participates in a business. The question is also whether to permanently pull the plug, or to put the project, programme or participation on hold and revisit it at a later date. I suppose all research and development-oriented organizations face this challenge.

In its history, Reliance Life Sciences has pulled the plug on several projects—those that did not make progress, were burning money or could not achieve their desired outcomes. These projects ranged from process development for indigo, medicinal and aromatics plant extracts business, phage display to agro-based food products.

This is not easy, to say the least. It is a painful process. One has to deal with acceptance of market or business realities, stifling human aspirations, facing financial write-offs and posting losses, re-assigning responsibilities, wounding egos, and suggesting graceful exits, to outright disengagement. There are no stock solutions.

CREATIVE DESTRUCTION

Pulling the plug on a programme or project pales in comparison to entire sites or businesses being taken out. When a new business takes its place, it amounts to creative destruction. For long-term sustenance, businesses sometimes have to go through such a metamorphosis. There are several examples in nature to substantiate this, e.g. the campus of Reliance Life Sciences at Navi Mumbai came out of an approach of 'Ringing out the old, ringing in the new.'

The Reliance group has had an ethos of creative destruction. Some sites or buildings are completely taken down. New ones are then built, which are far more modern and evolved, flexible and consistent with business demands. Apart from Reliance Life Sciences, examples of creative destruction include the Reliance Corporate Park and the revamped HN Reliance Foundation Hospital.

Such situations are very challenging because what goes down are not just facilities and businesses, but also the careers of individuals involved, aspirations of family members and their anchor to a place and community. During such times, one approach is to be dispassionate. A better approach is to balance the humanitarian outlook with the company's larger interest.

DEALING WITH INTEGRITY ISSUES

However, when there are integrity issues with a research project, a programme, or an individual, there has to be an outright dispassionate disengagement. There is no place for emotive connect with the individual, and separation is carried out like a surgical excision. This is relatively easy to decide but has to be done quickly and gracefully.

In our early days on the HN Hospital campus, we did face an issue of misrepresentation in science. A reported discovery turned out to be false. It was based on manipulation of gel pictures. Fortunately for us, it was discovered before it was published thanks to the alertness and questioning by a senior colleague. Without hesitation, we asked the senior scientist at fault to leave the company the very same day.

In another instance, we found out that another scientist did not have a doctoral degree as claimed. We informed the university concerned and did not hesitate to cut the chord with the scientist. In a third instance, a medical doctor was found to have resorted to financial irregularities. It met with the same organizational response—dismissal.

Another time, a senior colleague who was bringing in good business was found to be behaving inappropriately with a woman team member and was shown the door the same day. Reliance Life Sciences also had a few cases of manipulation of travel expenses. In such instances, the concerned individual was packed off the very same day.

DEALING WITH FRAUD

Dealing quickly and decisively with fraud involving finance, as well as dealing with criminal behaviour, can be very challenging. The biggest challenge in pulling the plug on a person and/ or a team that Reliance Life Sciences has faced was in the context of a large exposure to the pharmaceuticals business. In November 2006, Reliance Life Sciences hired a very senior professional from a large Indian pharmaceutical company to start a pharmaceutical business. This hiring was at a very high cost disproportionate to our norms and I was not in favour of it.

Subsequently, an independent company was formed within the larger ambit of the life sciences business, and the pharmaceutical business head set up a new team, hiring individuals he had been previously associated with. This team was housed in a different location in the city. A large budget was sanctioned for the project, based on a large generic pharmaceutical company model with manufacturing, to be set up in Jamnagar, in a Special Economic Zone.

Soon enough, I was alerted by Anand Vaze, head of capital procurement, to some unnerving developments. The formulations manufacturing head of the pharmaceutical company and two team members independently reporting to the new business head, were found to have links with some vendors to whom big purchase commitments were made. In return, favours were taken from vendors during their overseas travel. It's a small world of vendors in this business. We investigated more and Anand Vaze's suspicions were confirmed. I confronted the pharmaceutical business head and suggested that the formulations manufacturing head and his two team members should go. I was surprised by the business head's immediate consent. We sacked the three employees.

To me, if anyone casts an aspersion on my team member, I ask for some time, place the team member under watch, look for telltale signs of inappropriate behaviour and try to find evidence to validate the suspicion.

I reported this to Mukesh Ambani. He said, 'Fine, you did the right thing.' I responded that it was not exactly fine by me and narrated the readiness of the business head to sack two colleagues whom he had hired. 'Anyone else would have wanted to know more, given time to get into specifics and then got back with their views,' I said. I also told him of my discomfort with this team being located in a different place. Mukesh Ambani responded by saying that I should bring them in my line of sight. Soon, we shifted the entire team to the life sciences campus, much to the discomfort of the business head.

Having the pharmaceutical business head and the small team in the same campus gave us more visibility. Once we had a joint meeting near Frankfurt. While a colleague and I travelled directly from Mumbai to Frankfurt, the pharmaceutical business head left a day earlier and came via Zurich to meet us at Frankfurt airport. I found this detour unusual. I had his past overseas travel details examined and found that every overseas trip by the business head was made via Zurich. I brought this to Mukesh Ambani's attention.

In September 2008, during the global financial meltdown, Reliance Industries Limited faced the heat with business prospects dipping. It was decided to conserve cash and wind down open positions. After several weeks of reviews and assessing exposures, we changed the business model of the pharmaceutical business, from its large, generic pharmaceutical company model, to a later-generation, small-molecule, generic oncology products-based business model.

By that time, significant commitments had been made. A large amount of equipment, including several high-speed filling lines, had been ordered. Engineering consultants had been engaged. Civil construction had progressed rapidly. A bigger team was on board. Synthetic chemistry research work had started. A small active pharmaceutical ingredients facility had been built. A cold decision was made to rationalize—it was not a full-scale abort, but a substantial one.

I was tasked to carry out this transition, in addition to the biotechnology engagement in life sciences. Rahul Padhye willingly took over the task of heading the reformatted business. The business head and a few senior heads were requested to find other opportunities, which they did. Other key resources were either retained or re-allocated in Reliance Life Sciences. The independent pharmaceutical company, as well as the biopharmaceuticals, clinical research and diagnostics groups were merged into Reliance Life Sciences.

As part of the post-separation diligence, Rahul checked all the records of the pharmaceutical business head. One evening, as I was on my way back home from a meeting at Maker Chambers, he called me and broke the news that the business head was suspected to have committed financial fraud and siphoned off money. We did a full-scale internal investigation into the matter and looked at electronic records and trails. It soon became clear that the scale of the financial fraud was about two million US dollars.

I talked to Mukesh Ambani and suggested filing a criminal complaint with the police. We did this and after a year-long judicial process, recovered all the embezzled money. We were able to recover the money thanks to the quiet persuasiveness of a select group of our functional leads, supported by the legal counsel for the Reliance group. A settlement deed was filed in the Bombay High Court to recover the money. The entire process involved painstaking work, persistence, maintaining confidentiality, and above all, enduring high levels of stress. To Mukesh Ambani's credit, he acknowledged that I was right in my suspicions in the first instance.

The legal counsel of the Reliance group and a senior finance head were strongly in favour of going to the media with a press release, on the day the business head was taken into custody. I was not at all in favour of this, as it would have been detrimental to the process of recovering the money. We would be bogged down by media queries and would have to spend a lot of time and effort to address them.

I sought Mukesh Ambani's intervention. He was busy with a Reliance Innovation Council meeting in Jamnagar and knew that I would bother him only if I had no other option left. He held a conference call with me, the corporate legal counsel and the corporate finance head and heard our views on the matter. In the end, Mukesh Ambani said that he agreed with me and that going to the media did not make any sense. The matter ended there.

An important lesson from this incident is that rushing to the media does not always help, particularly for sensitive matters. In fact, it can complicate matters—the more sensationalist the story, the greater the chance of not getting the desired outcome. Most people do not understand that media exposure can take you to a high, but it can also bring you crashing down very quickly.

In another, but relatively smaller instance of financial fraud, the sudden change in lifestyle of a colleague in accounting triggered our suspicions. We were able to detect the fraud quickly, and recovered the money involved in an overnight operation. When I reported the matter to Mukesh Ambani the next day, he promptly appreciated that we had acted as company owners would have done. He had the right to castigate us for our lack of intensive controls, but did not do so. From all this, I have come to appreciate the need for keeping key persons in the line of sight, ensuring that financial controls are in place, trusting individuals based only on long-term engagements, and taking immediate and decisive action with the help of a multi-faceted competent task force constituted for the purpose.

FINANCIAL CHECKS AND BALANCES

In my experience, well-run organizations have strong financial checks and balances, and depend on the quality of their people, systems and processes. They provide limited latitude to key leadership, with a strong oversight. Most organizations that have gone down the tube have not had such oversight; hence, there have been problems with rogue traders, internal banking fraudsters and corrupt decision-makers.

Sometimes you have pseudo organizational evangelists who propagate a culture of self-control for employees. Sooner or later, this results in fraud in the organization. To my mind, self-control is a myth. Human beings have desires. The nature and extent of these desires, as well as the points in time that such desires come up, vary.

REGULATORY EXASPERATION

If talent has been the greatest challenge for Reliance Life Sciences, the regulatory environment has been the biggest source of frustration. India inherited a bureaucracy that was designed to serve a colonial ruler's interest of controlling a large populace, spread over a large mass of land, in a distant place. I must give credit to the British, who, with limited resources, were able to control vast parts of the world. Likewise, credit is also to the Spanish, French and Portuguese who had their colonies. What helped them was the bureaucracy that they created to rule from a distant land, serving their purpose. But continuance of the bureaucratic system beyond the exit of the colonial masters is detrimental, to say the least.

Describing the bureaucracy in India in all its detail can take up many pages. Suffice it is to say that today, it has become a prisoner of its past, with bureaucrats belonging to a privileged class. In the Indian bureaucracy, access to resources—human, material, financial and time—is assumed. Financial needs are taken care of by levying more taxes, duties and levies on a select few. These taxes are levied on people who are already burdened by direct and indirect taxes. Direct taxes, such as income tax, are visible and largely known to the taxpayer. Indirect taxes, such as sales tax, turnover tax, customs duties, excise duties, cess and other levies, are hidden in the retail prices and charged to not so well-informed buyers. Not many appreciate the value for time and respect for investments at stake by the investor. Translated into practice, what an investor, an entrepreneur or a citizen gets is a maze of rules, regulations and implied threats to take punitive action.

From the bureaucracy, you will rarely get a clear articulation of what is required for an approval. You will rarely get to know what sequence of steps will be followed. You will invariably never get an opportunity for consultation and guidance or a commitment to time-bound approvals. Save for a few exceptions, the judicial process is used more for thwarting and delaying justice.

Expert committees and advisory boards have come to be the preserve of a privileged few from academic, research and healthcare institutions. Some individuals on these committees and boards tend to make value judgements, sometimes have a conflict of interest, demand standards that their own institutions do not have and, above all, have a tendency to pontificate.

In the biotechnology space, Reliance Life Sciences has had

to contend with a flood of queries posed by reviewers. Obscure regulations, especially in stem cells therapeutics, have virtually ended the emergence of India as a leader in this area. Due to manpower limitations, regulatory audits take very long to be scheduled and, when they are conducted, it takes a long time for reports to be prepared. Sometimes, non-scientific demands are made for additional studies. A series of queries is generated and frequent changes are made in data requirements. Clinical trial and marketing approvals have no defined processes and time frames. Above all, approval letters are issued much after verbal approvals are given in a meeting.

When it comes to the testing of product batches at national laboratories, our experience has been that referrals are made by regulators without checking if these laboratories have the infrastructure, competent staff, standard operating procedures, antibodies, reagents, consumables, and independent accreditations from reputed international bodies. These laboratories also do not admit their inability to test a particular product. As a result they depend on our standard operating procedures, want us to train their human resources, supply reagents, antibodies, consumables and lend analysts. Sometimes they ask for additional tests not warranted by science. In this process, time periods for testing and release get unduly extended, much to the cost and discomfort of the manufacturer.

The pharmaceutical industry in India is also faced with the same set of issues except that the gestation periods are relatively shorter. Several types of approvals have been decentralized and are now issued by state agencies that have widely varying requirements and approval times. The fractured nature of the industry has caught regulators in an activity trap of constantly issuing licences and permits. It has also fostered fly-by-night operators. These operators revel in the infirmities of archaic systems and processes.

Reliance Life Sciences and many others in our industry

have endured this with a 'squirm and bear it' attitude. We are left making a 'noise' now and then, which has served no useful purpose. We have learnt to manage with uncertainty. We eternally long for freedom from such regulations. It is like the ox, in historical times, going round and round the oil mill, from dawn to dusk, day after day, waiting for freedom.

PILGRIMS' TRAVAILS

The effort you have to make to meet regulators is akin to going on a pilgrimage to a holy place of worship. It requires periodic travel to regulators' offices in Mumbai, Navi Mumbai and Delhi, where, armed with a wish list, you have to spend long hours waiting for an appointment or waiting for the start of a meeting.

What took the cake was when my colleagues went for a subject experts committee meeting following a formal invitation. After waiting for the whole day for their turn on the agenda, they were told that they had been called by mistake. There was no word of apology and no concern for the manpower and travel costs, let alone the cost of time wasted in waiting. The pilgrims' travails continue.

SEEING GHOSTS

As if our exasperation with the regulatory system was not enough, Reliance Life Sciences also had to contend with some colleagues interpreting regulations in their own way. This often created impediments. The common refrain would be, 'Regulators won't approve of this.' This statement would be made with such aplomb that not many in the room would challenge it. With regulators not being very accessible or forthcoming, and with no system of formal consultation, such ghost visualizers had a field day.

Being a novice, initially I was carried away by such

statements. Then I started to see a pattern in the raising of imaginary regulatory red flags by managers, whom we refer to as 'RLS' own super regulators.' Some of us would then ask these managers for specific information from the statutory acts or case law reports. Often, their contentions would be proven unfounded. The problem is that nobody wants to write to, or meet with, a regulator and ask for clarifications.

Reliance Life Sciences probably lost about a year because of the ghost visualizers within the organization. A few clinical trials were delayed for submission because of a notion that the regulator would ask for different data. In another case, contract manufacturing was delayed because of a false belief that regulators would not allow biopharmaceutical contract manufacturing. After careful study, it emerged that nowhere in the Drugs and Cosmetics Act was it stated that contract manufacturing of biopharmaceuticals could not be done. We applied and we did get the approval.

In another instance, we applied for registering an imported product. We were advised to submit it as a request for a No Objection Certificate (NOC) to one agency. After repeated follow-up, we were told to apply to another agency for an NOC! After a long gap, we were told to file for product registration as well. So we had to chase bureaucrats and regulators for two pending applications for the same requirement.

SPECIAL FORCE

For us as upstarts, the markets were a big challenge. The basic business model of Reliance Life Sciences envisages the treating physician or surgeon as the primary customer, the patient as the secondary customer and the hospital buyer and pharmacy heads as tertiary customers. This was because of the nature of our products and the fact that these services were highly differentiated from small molecule generic drugs, and catered to super specialty doctors. In the early days, doctors had a sense of disbelief that Reliance could be in the life sciences business. Many doctors would dismiss us as non-serious players. But this did not deter us.

Reliance Infocomm was launched in December 2002 with a pan-India initiative in mobile phone services based on CDMA technology. This initiative revolutionized telecommunications in India, based as it was on a ubiquitous network and services offered at very aggressive prices that were a fraction of those offered by incumbents. Many doctors had bought mobile phones and had some teething issues given the massive scale-up of subscribers in a very short period of time. The moment a Reliance Life Sciences executive walked in, they would simply hand over the phone and ask for a resolution of their problem, before entertaining the executive for the planned promotional activity.

To their credit, business executives, area managers and sales and marketing heads of Reliance Life Sciences would make sincere efforts to help colleagues in Reliance Infocomm, who were actually inundated with such requests. In many cases, I would have such issues resolved too. Grateful doctors would then be all ears for Reliance Life Sciences' executives.

The persistence of our marketing team members and their willingness to help, enabled us to gain credibility with doctors in a convoluted, but effective way. An important learning has been to pay attention to a customer's requirement, even if, at times, it pertains to something not related to your product-market context.

Then came the challenge of spreading our message in relatively newer domains such as molecular medicine, regenerative medicine and biotherapeutics. In the first instance, marketing executives had to be trained extensively, which we did and continue to do, to this day. Thereafter, medical doctors had to be met and key messages communicated in such a way that they were understood easily. Medical seminars were held frequently for this purpose.

With some products, such as fibrin sealants, executives had to actually stand in operating theatres with the appropriate operating room attire, and assist the surgeon and operating room nurses in using the product. Calls for assistance from operating room staff would come at odd hours. The executives had to thaw the product in warm water baths at the right time, and re-constitute and prepare the applicator that docked twin syringes in a mixer. Many of these executives were entering an operating room for the first time. A few of them reported feeling giddy. At the end of the day, customers were won over with a strong value proposition. This was based on assessing the value for doctors, patients and hospitals in such aspects as efficacy, adverse events, costs, hospital stay period, treatment time, operating time, recovery time, clear field of view in surgery, loss of blood, and so on. On the ground, this was supported by a well-debated unique selling proposition, key messages and a stratified customer list. It was supported by a distribution system that enabled us to make the product available to the hospital or to the patient's relative at the right time.

Today, Reliance Life Sciences reaches out to patients, hospitals and doctors across India on the strength of its marketing force, which is not an army of soldiers as in the big pharmaceutical companies, but a special force—trained, skilled, technology-enabled and with the capability to win against odds. The team has among the highest sales force productivity levels in the industry.

MINDING MINDSETS

The old adage 'You can take a horse to the water but you cannot make it drink', comes to mind when I deal with some mindsets in Reliance Life Sciences. While a horse will drink when it gets thirsty, you can't say the same for humans. Mindsets change only after continuously working on them. We have often confronted mindset issues that manifest in such statements as 'This is difficult to achieve', 'This is impossible', 'This is not the way it is done', 'In my former company, we would do it this way and therefore, we should do it this way now', 'The regulators would not approve of this', 'This is inconsistent with our policy', 'In this company, there is a command and control in operation and nothing will change.'

Two examples will help to illustrate this point. At one stage, when we were limited by plasma availability to manufacture plasma proteins, the common refrain among my marketing colleagues was, 'We could have got more revenues if we had stocks of albumin.' Marketing professionals have a way of highlighting products with constrained availability, not products where availability is not a constraint.

We thought to ourselves about what would happen if we had no plasma at all. This led us to question why we had to be dependent on our own research and development efforts. Marketing was encouraged to think of Reliance Life Sciences as one production source and to see which other external products we could source in partnership. Not that this was a new concept. All that it reflects is that when we get engaged intensively with what we have set out to do, we often do not see choices outside our boundaries.

A not-so-apt, but adequate analogy in this context is of childless women going through repeated and unsuccessful fertility treatment cycles when the option of adoption exists. Likewise, mothers who want to have more children but have had medical issues, do not want to go through the hardships of pregnancy and resort to adoption, thus having both biological and adopted children.

The second example is related to seeing beyond one's boundaries. We did face issues in getting regulatory approvals. I applied the same principle when Jamila Joseph, head of clinical research, would express her frustration with long delays with regulators. We agreed that each business is free to use external service providers for support functions that we have internally, instead of being limited by internal capabilities. The underlying principle was that the external service provider option can be exercised only where there was a clear cost, time and quality advantage. This has started to play out.

External recourse to research, product development, product supply, manufacturing, services and support functions inherently challenge internal teams. This has to be exercised judiciously to balance motivation of internal teams and organizational imperatives. An open and transparent communication can help placate internal teams affected by such outsourcing.

VALUE JUDGEMENTS

Another mindset is related to making value judgements. Many of us make remarks or voice opinions that are not founded on facts. It is a natural human trait and we need to constantly remind ourselves to avoid making value judgements. In building the life sciences business, I have come across value judgements being made during interviews of candidates, in annual performance appraisals and in dealing with difficult colleagues.

When I assess the performance of those who respond directly to me and write down my comments, I filter my assessment through several screens, asking myself questions such as: Is what I have written based on facts? Has it been influenced by recent events or performance? Is it free from emotional reasoning? Am I overplaying one aspect over the other? Am I being fair?

All this is not just a comment on others, but, equally, of me. Sometimes I do have a tendency to make a value judgement in a situation or in relation to a person. But I try to correct myself and make it a point to apologize. For example, one principle that I have found useful is to sleep over an issue that I am dealing with, more so when it involves negativity, and think about the situation dispassionately the next day. Invariably, I would have either a moderated view or a different perspective of the situation. I suppose most leaders go through this process in their minds.

Dealing with mindset and value judgement challenges is easier said than done. It needs constant application of the mind, a conviction that things can be done differently, an act of taking a step back and looking at first principles and concepts involved, and a sense of being responsible for others. Constant communication is one way in which you can deal with mindset-related challenges, both for yourself and for others, and bring about better performance.

I regularly make two-hour presentations on soft skills development at our monthly retreats. I find these presentations very useful in sensitizing colleagues about changing mindsets, being good leaders, not making value judgements and improving personality traits. Frequent review meetings, interactions in smaller groups and one-on-one conversations are opportunities for developing deeper perspectives and better understanding. During these conversations, I often think of parallels, sometimes humorous ones, to drive home the point. This strategy has indeed been effective.

I use so many analogies that I can fill an entire book with them. A select few examples are given below:

- Good leaders working successfully on multiple programmes, projects, manufacturing batches, clinical trials and product launches are like jugglers in a circus. They need strong focus all the time and eyes constantly on all the objects in the air. The more the objects, the greater the intensity and energy required.
- A salesperson unable to describe the status of a product at any given time, is akin to parents who have many children and are unable to recall which school a

particular child goes to, or even which grade the child studies in.

- A manufacturing batch that goes well but fails in bacterial endotoxin tests is analogous to a stillborn child and has to be scrapped. Months of effort end in disappointment and sorrow.
- For a product manager, every product is like his or her baby. It has to be carefully nurtured and provided all the resources needed to grow and develop. The market cannot be blamed for failures. The extent of care and the resources provided for growth, are the real issues. But many people tend to blame external factors instead of looking within.
- Efforts that do not result in outcomes are the equivalent of 'operation successful, patient dead.' Doctors and hospitals may be happy, but the patient or the patients' near and dear ones, are not. Likewise, in the case of a brilliant experiment that does not result in anything of value—the scientist and the research team may be happy, but not the organization.

WORLDLY VOYAGES

At Reliance Life Sciences, the thrust on globalization remains a daunting challenge. There are multiple models of globalization—home-based exporting, setting shop on overseas shores, partnering with local, regional or global players, getting a strategic regional or global investor, to name a few—which can be used in the following contexts: research and/or technology access, product markets, contracting, funding, hiring, legal liabilities, tax planning, and ensuring quality.

Reliance Life Sciences recognized early on that it can do product development and conduct pre-clinical and clinical studies to generate data in the Indian context, while manufacturing in some of the world markets. We realized that we did not have the ability, financial strength or depth of talent to conduct clinical trials in the US, European Union (EU), Japan and other complex markets, go through a regulatory approval process, understand the nuances of marketing, deal with issues around quality and public liability, and respond to entrenched competitive practices. Thus, out-licensing partnerships emerged as an avenue to participate in developed markets and larger regional ones.

Where products or services had to be developed and delivered in India, we would do it on our own, such as with domestic medical marketing, inbound clinical research services, contract research and contract manufacturing services. However, this was not cast in stone. Beyond a point, when we were keen on scaling up, we did open up to 'principal to principal relationships', or P2P, but with limited exclusivity, to mean only the partner company and Reliance Life Sciences, in the Indian market. In this way, we thought that we could leverage the marketing reach of the big Indian pharmaceutical companies, as they were fond of claiming to have thousands of field sales force personnel reaching almost every nook and corner of India.

The experience here has been mixed. A leading Indian pharmaceutical company could not meet product uptake commitments for a recombinant hormone product, even after we gave the company some latitude. They gracefully exited the contract after buying the rest of the year's commitment. In another case, a smaller company gave a relatively large order for a plasma protein product and a recombinant product. Probably, they bit off far more than they could chew and never came back. The best experience we have had is with a multinational pharmaceutical company in India and another large Indian pharmaceutical company. Both of them built volumes and continue to be regular customers, keeping both their volume and payment commitments.

For products, not services, that would go to the rest of the world, we would either market them on our own label or that of distributors, whichever made sense, and have a local partner to support participation in the tender and trade segments of the business in those countries. Inherently, we would be limited by the motivation and ability of our partners. In larger regional markets, like Russia/CIS, Brazil, and developed markets, we were clear about the need to forge partnerships defining roles and responsibilities based on where our strengths were. This has started playing out and will be a major growth driver in the near-term and long-term.

DAVID VS GOLIATH

In forging such global partnerships, we initially tried to reach out to larger global pharmaceutical and biotechnology companies. On two occasions, Reliance Life Sciences did engage with global investment banks on a pure success fee basis and reimbursement of pre-approved costs, to find such partners. The experience was disappointing.

We would have several rounds of discussions with potential partners, spread over many months, only to be given a reason to walk away. Such reasons ranged from board of directors' disapproval, products not within strategic business focus, change in strategy, preference for late stage development or that a decision was taken only when the product was close to marketing after regulatory approval. Most of these pushbacks could have been avoided had the potential partner been clear about the determinants for in-licensing to begin with.

To illustrate, with two big global pharmaceutical companies, we spent months in discussions with all the key members of their respective executive management teams. One was in Germany and the other in the US. Product testing was also done by one company and there was satisfaction on all parameters, but in the end, we were told by both companies that the board was not supportive. The reason given was the high investments involved in clinical development in the US and EU.

Our sense was that each company was unclear about entering into the biosimilars business. It was not a question of financial resources or clinical development and regulatory skills. A few years later, both these companies entered the biosimilars business. The Indian entity of one of these companies also wanted to partner with us for other world markets.

Another major US-based pharmaceutical company told us at their American headquarters that they would be interested only if we had a product close to be launched after regulatory approvals. We were informed about this after a few rounds of discussions and email exchanges, and were left wondering about their risk-taking ability. At that time, the regulatory pathway in the US for biosimilars marketing approval was obscure.

On the surface, these reasons may sound credible. However, in some cases, we did have suspicions that the discussions with Reliance Life Sciences could have been motivated by several aspects, from seeking competitive intelligence, to confused thinking, to the aspirations of a small team and not the larger organization.

An interesting aspect is that the big biotechnology companies would dislike being told that they were confused. Initially, they started by saying that there is no such thing as a biosimilar and used lobbying organizations to put forth such a view in the US. This met with much success in delaying biosimilars legislation. Probably they took this position in order to protect their high-cost, high-yield secure turfs.

At one conference, the moderator of my panel confused my name with that of my twin brother. When my turn came, I said, 'The moderator has confused my name with that of my brother. It is fine with me because my brother and I are like biosimilars. The biotechnology innovators may not subscribe to this.' There was great amusement among audience members. I am sure that the big biotech boys in the room must have been hiding their scorn. Much later, many of these companies started their own biosimilar outfits. Today, with a rare exception or two, all of them participate in the biosimilars business.

The big pharmaceutical companies, both global and Indian, were no better. They were unclear about their biosimilars strategy. Some of them in India ventured into it and were either late in the race or failed. The big global investment banks did no better. They would start by making sales pitches about their unique access to the top management. Soon, we would be dealing with some middle level talent in these banks and plodding our way through with no success until we would call it off.

One challenge that we faced in dealing with global multinational pharmaceutical companies is that it would take months to even set up a meeting by our investment bank partners. This happened because teams of the multinational company from different parts of the world would be involved. Every key person or nominee would have to find the time, and a common schedule would have to be agreed among them. Inherently, the bureaucracy of a large organization would slow things down—all this, even though we made the effort and took time out to meet them in their global headquarters in the US or Europe. The gap between two meetings was long, and sooner or later, we would run out of patience despite the promise of potential scale that such a partnership would provide. Agility mattered more to us than size.

From our experience, we found that what matters is the burning desire of a potential partner to progress and see a partnership with Reliance as a means to progress. Companies that saw their growth in our growth, and where we saw our growth in the partner's growth, were the best bet. David mattered more than Goliath. Those who dared, triumphed.

12

FENDING FOR ONESELF

'A product in scarcity is more
demanding than one in surplus.'

*Many find it hard to believe that it is far more difficult to
deal with products that are critical to society, being in shortage
than in surplus. Conventional schools of thought and training
do not dwell on the challenges in marketing a product in a
shortage situation.*

*Challenges in selling a product in a dire shortage revolve
around how to keep consumers' interests uppermost at all
times, ensuring there are no corrupt practices by customer-
facing persons within the organization and among business
associates, dealing with pressure groups, dealing with
aggressive media, getting policy planners to act, and sourcing
raw materials in a critical supply situation; all of this, within
a narrow window of time.*

*During such times it is tempting to do piggyback selling.
This involves pushing other products that are in surplus on
the back of products in short supply. It may work in the short
run, but backfires in the long run.*

*Ironically, during such times, many guns are trained on
the organization that continues to supply, for shortfalls in*

supplies, while letting off those who failed to supply. Lip service would be paid for support sought to alleviate the shortage situation. In the end, there is a realization that one has to fend for oneself in managing the situation.

ALBUMIN SHORTAGE

In late 2014, India experienced a shortage of albumin, a plasma protein product. By then, Reliance Life Sciences was the largest manufacturer of plasma proteins in India, with a dominant market share. We saw the shortage looming on the horizon. Our US-based primary raw material supplier had started to scale back their yearly commitments to us. However, they had a strong business ethic of honouring commitments to the last kilogram. For quite some time we had been working on prospecting for alternative import options. We were able to tie up with a few foreign sources. The global plasma proteins industry is an oligopoly with a limited number of players. We were the new kids in town on the fringes of entering this limited club. Our entry, therefore, did cause curiosity and concern among entrenched industry players.

The shortage situation was getting aggravated. Chinese consumption was growing rapidly. US demand was recovering. This was compounded when the Indian government brought a number of products under price control, including albumin. The opportunistic players quit. They were typically importers of final products. So were transnational companies that used to sell albumin when they had a surplus in their home markets or other preferred markets. Consequently, the Indian albumin market was left with only three players - Reliance Life Sciences as a large manufacturer, a recent entrant with a small facility in Hyderabad and a transnational company that continued to sell, but with lower quantities.

We were probably the only company to have expressed in writing to Indian regulatory authorities that we were fine with price control on albumin as long as it was not reduced further. This was based on our competitive advantage and, above all, our commitment to India. We expressed our commitment to produce and supply, as well as to expand our manufacturing capacity as long as the government could help us access more plasma from within India—from government supported blood banks—and give us fast-track permits to import plasma. The government took very long to respond to our first request, while with the second one, the response was erratic and there was a very long processing time, running into months.

DEALING WITH SHORTAGE

We then worked on getting regulatory approvals for imports. Now, this is a long and arduous process for biologicals. We increased our trips to Delhi to meet regulatory agencies to expedite approvals for imports. We highlighted the shortage situation and expressed the commitment of Reliance Life Sciences to continue to manufacture and supply albumin. We also wrote, more than once, that we could produce more if import approvals were given, and applied for an emergency approval.

But few government officials cared to listen to our requests. The bureaucratic machinery was not oriented to respond to shortage situations, going by our experience with albumin. To add salt to injury, the price control authority in India, the National Pharmaceutical Pricing Authority (NPPA), sent letters asking us to supply albumin in areas where there were shortages. Periodically, this authority would ask us how much we had supplied. We responded to every single letter from the authority. I once asked an NPPA official why the NPPA was not chasing those who quit the market and prevail upon them to supply albumin. He had no answer.

Every other day, we would get desperate requests from the family members of patients for a few bottles of albumin. These patients usually were in intensive care units and needed urgent infusions, but the product was not available in the hospitals. Many of these requests also came through Reliance group colleagues. Some of these colleagues had turned their backs on us in the past when Reliance Life Sciences had sought their assistance. Requests would also come in from external contacts, including drug regulatory officials themselves. Sometimes, these requests would come at odd hours. We could understand the anxiety and desperation that made these people reach out to us at such late hours, and made sure that every request was addressed. In the case of albumin, doctors do have the less effective medical option of plasma infusion instead of albumin infusion.

Based on our retail drug licence, the marketing team made limited stocks available at our head office to cater directly to the needs of patients in the vicinity. In other locations, supplies were made through the nearest business associates. The marketing team had a policy of dealing with requests for emergency supplies of products in short supply. Under this well-defined process, only the company president could authorize the issue of a product in times of shortage. We had to take a cautious approach to repeat requests and endeavoured to satisfy the maximum number of needy patients.

Every single member in the sales team was cautioned that if he or she was found to have been involved in any inappropriate transaction, their services would be terminated the same day. Similar action would be taken in situations involving fraudulent claims, indiscipline and inappropriate behavior, particularly with women employees. Business associates were informed well in advance that if anyone was found diverting a shortage product to the grey market, their contract would be terminated. Reliance Life Sciences also made every attempt to get maximum yields from every drop of input raw material. This included incremental process improvements. It also involved investing in additional facilities to get albumin from several intermediate products.

It is only during shortages that individuals, organizational units and societies understand the value of resources. For us in Reliance Life Sciences, productivity—materials, capital, human and information—has always been paramount. Material productivity was even more important in a shortage situation.

REVERBERATIONS

We made sure that albumin bottles were not available for traders, who grew very unhappy with Reliance Life Sciences. They were losing an opportunity to sell albumin at very high prices in the grey market. We also carefully monitored stock movement to ensure that hospitals would get the product whenever possible. Monthly stock verification would be done at the warehouses of business associates. Distribution trade associations went to the media. We responded to every media query. They seemed to have given up.

Reliance Life Sciences instituted all these measures to ensure that patients did not suffer in a situation of shortage. Even before price control came into force, Reliance Life Sciences had the lowest maximum retail prices of albumin in India. This is true for almost all our products that are not under price control. Reliance Life Sciences could do this as its products were hospital products and differentiated in nature. Distribution trade associations in India do have a history of having brought big pharmaceutical companies to their knees. They did this by imposing a ban on carrying the concerned pharmaceutical companies' products at the distributor, wholesale and retail chemist levels.

Most competitors would keep the maximum retail prices very high, so that there was greater incentive for hospitals and distribution channel partners to make money. Some competitors even went to the extent of spreading stories among doctors linking the lower prices of our products to poorer quality. This was done with a mala fide intention. In effect, these competitors were placing a fig leaf over their own high product prices. But gullible doctors got taken in, until we were able to clarify the matter.

Reliance Life Sciences faced all these challenges in the interest of patients; and, equally, in the interest of greater affordability and accessibility of our products. We were clear from the beginning of our journey that, to succeed in the Indian market, you have to get the price-volume tradeoff right. In contrast, traders and overseas companies exporting to India had no such concern or responsibility.

DIFFERENT WORLDS

Government officials were occupied with relatively more pressing concerns. They would typically deal with situations only when the pressure was at its maximum. I have often shared this perspective with progressive-minded drug regulators, who agreed with me. Such progressive regulators also felt that this way of working could get corrected by creating an independent unified drug regulatory authority. Such an authority should not have ex-officio administrative cadre officials, but competent technical, financial, legal, social science, industry and ethics professionals. Many committees have recommended this, but the administrative services probably did not want to lose control and have not let this happen. An independent drug authority can respond to shortage situations in quick time, as is evident from the regulatory system in the US.

DIFFERENT STROKES

A drug product going into shortage can evoke a variety of human reactions. From my experience, there is an inverse correlation between income levels and intention to pay when it comes to the shortage of a drug product. The well-off shop around for discounts. The less privileged are keener to get their hands on the product and are willing to pay whatever it costs. The well-connected want someone else to pay for it.

PARADOX OF MARKETING

In my view, it is far more difficult to sell products in shortage than to sell products in surplus supply, though marketing folks may not agree with me. When I first shared my views about the challenges in marketing a product in a shortage situation with my marketing colleagues, they looked at me strangely. Today, all of them realize, in the wake of the albumin shortage, that they are better off selling a product that is in surplus.

The challenges in selling a product that is in a dire shortage revolve around keeping the consumer's interests top of mind at all times, dealing with pressure groups, dealing with aggressive media, getting policy planners to act, sourcing raw materials in a critical supply situation; all of this, within a narrow window of time. During such times, it is tempting to do piggyback selling. This involves pushing other products that are in surplus on the back of products in short supply. It may work in the short run, but backfires in the long run.

In May 2009, after we had launched erythropoietin and were faced with slower sales, we took recourse to selling erythropoietin on the back of other fast-moving products. Our business associates were very unhappy. To deal with this, many of them took a 'haircut' on their margins and sold one or more of their other products to hospitals, at cheaper prices. Erythropoietin's secondary sales did not improve much, but overall we faced a difficult pricing situation. Then, the pushback came in terms of delayed payments and bounced cheques and soon enough, we had debtors to deal with.

We overcame the situation with stronger communications and intensive monitoring of collections. We continue to focus on strong communications and relationships and focus on sustained collections, even though the storm had passed many years ago. Today the product sells large volumes on its own standing in an intensely competitive market.

LIP SERVICE

Working with the biofuels farm advocacy team, led by Sudarshan Srinivas, took me to the rural hinterlands in India where I had the opportunity to see and relate to the ground realities. Chasing the agriculture initiative with Pascal Noronha and his team gave me insights into agriculture. I realized the risks that a farmer faces in India. Working with Pascal Noronha and the Jamnagar greenbelt development team gave me insights into farming techniques and the economics of scale in farming.

While at Indian Petrochemicals Corporation Limited, I had the opportunity to support, during my leisure hours, the initiatives of Dr Sunil Desai and C. Sadanandan and his team as part of a social development organization. This organization helped Karodia village, in Baroda district, in Gujarat, improve its school infrastructure and provided healthcare services. This exposed me to rural politics and to issues in social development at the village level.

All these experiences convinced me that, in India, policy planners mostly pay lip service to farmers. The Indian farmer takes the highest risks among all and suffers from a range of issues such as agro-climatic conditions, labour availability and cost, seed quality, fertilizer quality, agro-chemicals quality and market risks. At the end of all this, the farmer gets a fraction of the retail price. I was aghast when I once visited Manipur and was told that the farmer of pineapples got one-tenth of the retail price!

Indian patients are also subjected to several risks. With drugs, the risks are associated with availability, appropriateness, quality and prices. Then there are several irrational drug combinations in the market, as well as the easy availability of prescription drugs over the counter. With some doctors, it's about their lack of competence. With clinics and hospitals, there are high costs, lack of infection control and hygiene, unnecessary procedures and diagnostics being performed. With healthcare centres, maintenance of patient records is another issue with some doctors letting patients keep all their records while others keep loose sheets of paper with patient records.

Health policy planners believe that pharmaceutical companies overcharge for drugs, and thus institute higher levels of price control. But, if you analyse the total cost of hospitalization, which is huge, at the time of a patient's discharge, it is apparent that the drug cost is only a fraction of the total cost. This is especially true when a surgical procedure is involved or a medical device is used. So, the natural question is: where should the policy planner focus in order to regulate healthcare costs?

Like farmers, school teachers also get the short end of the stick, especially those in state government-aided and most non-aided private schools. Indian teachers in these categories are paid poorly, while private school owners charge exorbitant fees. The teachers remain stagnant for long years, both in their career paths and the curriculum that they have to teach. On top of it, they risk action against themselves for admonishing students, e.g. catching children copying in examinations lands them in long-winded legal redress processes. So they turn a blind eye to copying when it takes place in examinations. This situation is no different from the one individuals who come to the aid of road accident victims face. To add to the woes of teachers, they have to carry out election and national survey duties by compulsion, and their schedules for training and government duties often come up at the eleventh hour, throwing their vacation plans out of gear.

INCONSIDERATENESS

Albumin is one of the several drugs in shortage because of issues with manufacturers, demand-supply mismatches, scares created by some pharmaceutical companies and government policies. Then there are drugs that have inconsistent supplies. Even if drugs do not face shortage situations, their availability in rural areas is inconsistent. On top of this, even if drugs are available, there are chances that they could be spurious.

Government policies also lead to shortages. Reliance Life Sciences experienced a case of irrational pricing of human plasma derived anti-rabies immunoglobulin and anti-tetanus immunoglobulin. These life-saving products can be made from equine or human plasma. The raw material cost of equine sources is about one-tenth of that of human sources. These two immunoglobulins were brought under price control in the year 2014. Unfortunately, the calculation of ceiling prices took an arithmetic average of equine and human source products.

Overnight, the availability of the two immunoglobulins became an issue. Reliance Life Sciences had developed the process and was on the verge of launching plasma products after obtaining regulatory approvals. We put the launches on hold, and from November 2014, we regularly wrote to and met regulators on this issue, but corrections took a long time. All that we achieved was to lose a couple of kilograms running from one ministry and agency to another! We were getting fatigued and embarrassed to follow up repeatedly.

Every drug in shortage and every drug that faces inconsistent supplies provides an opportunity for traders to exploit and fleece patients. Proactive government policies can prevent shortages in many ways—from appropriate pricing, market interventions, proactive planning and support to domestic manufacturers.

During the ordeal that my family and I faced during the long years of maintaining my comatose younger brother Srinivas, we dealt with numerous issues related to drug availability, quality and prices. Therefore, I was determined that even in the worst of shortage situations, Reliance Life Sciences would not let patients be fleeced. My colleagues in leadership positions subscribe to this view and have been happy to live by it.

We even wrote to regulators and spoke to them to suggest the names of certain biological products facing shortage or supply inconsistency issues, which we could develop, manufacture and market. We haven't received a response to date. Nevertheless, we decided to work on a few products, and they are in the development stage. We also consider that developing novel therapeutic proteins to address the specific disease needs in the country is our contribution to society. But this journey is long and full of imponderables.

The social perspective is sadly missing in some public policies and in many industry practices. But, who cares?

13

WISDOM FROM ENCOUNTERS

'Sharing wisdom enhances value for all.'

Learning can, at best, be a reference. Aspects that we learn in the early part of our schooling, the fundamental concepts in basic and applied sciences, our understanding of the universe...are all relative. This is because new discoveries are regularly made in all physical and applied sciences, science and technology periodically come up with new innovations and methods, societies evolve and humanity's creativity continuously explores new frontiers. Wisdom is a product of learning from inheritance, teaching and experiences.

Consequently, in hindsight, any decision can be seen as a great one or plain stupid. But, anyone can be wise in hindsight. It therefore, becomes an imperative for all to share our learning in experiences in whatever modest form and medium. Then the collective value of a family, enterprise and community is enhanced.

WORK THE DETAILS

In Reliance, a leader's response of 'Leave it to me, I will get it done' when it comes to execution will be met with skepticism. Mukesh Ambani's response is likely to be, 'Tell me what exactly, how exactly, who are the persons responsible, and in what sequence?' He is likely to look into the minutest detail if he senses that things are not going on track, or if there is overconfidence. A meeting that starts by his saying, 'Let's spend five minutes...' can easily go on for five hours late into the night. This happened to the petroleum refinery projects in both phases, the information and communication initiative and the 4G wireless broadband project, where the stakes were very high.

In this regard, Reliance Life Sciences was no exception, although the stakes were far lower for the company in relation to the mainstream businesses of the Reliance group. Naturally, in developing the life sciences initiative and in building the campus, we had to work the details in every small manner conceivable. There were several revisions till we developed a good sense of what we wanted to do and what we wanted to build.

BUILD BRICK BY BRICK

A building is built brick by brick, a drawing line by line, a painting brush stroke by brush stroke, a movie frame by frame, a student lesson by lesson...and this book word by word. Considerable energy, engagement and effort go into a creation; over a long time and by several individuals and teams.

Reliance Life Sciences has been created, and continues to be created, molecule by molecule, protein by protein, customer by customer, product by product and team by team. The physical dimensions are measurable and tangible, not the enterprise and the extent of engagement. This process and the effort continue. The end is far beyond our visual range.

BODY WITHOUT A MIND

For Reliance, building a new business in completely uncharted territory was not easy. In an environment that places demands on capital productivity and detailed execution, it was that much more difficult. Add to this the fact that I was a greenhorn in biotechnology, and the challenge became greater. I had taken the safe option of starting in a modest way. My first step was to understand the science, technology and business context. In the next step, scale up. In that way, the stakes in investment in science and infrastructure were high and failures had a small and digestible impact.

Many observers in the industry could not reconcile themselves to this and considered anything that Reliance did as a huge potential threat. They believed that Reliance would develop every business on a large format in an expansive manner. Naturally, there was an expectation that the life sciences business would also shake the industry.

This set the critics' tails wagging. Soon enough, many in the industry figured out that Reliance Life Sciences was not to be in the big league. The imagined threat of Reliance's participation in biotechnology turned out to be unfounded. One biotechnology industry leader went to the extent of remarking, 'Reliance Life Sciences is like a body without a mind.' This remark did hurt us initially, but it helped us resolve to prove our critics wrong.

FLYING UNDER THE RADAR

When some external constituencies and many within Reliance realized that Reliance Life Sciences was not going to be a large-scale venture in the same way as the other businesses, they either ignored us or refused to deal with us. They believed our venture was not worth the effort. This was both a disadvantage and an advantage. Developing a business that was not big, as expected out of Reliance, was thus perceived as a conservative and defensive business strategy by many external constituencies. At the same time, it gave us an ability to 'fly under the radar' and focus on what we had to do.

Keeping a low profile and 'flying under the radar' emanated from a realization that there were many imponderables in biotechnology. Out of the many tasks you performed, some would succeed and others would fail. It was important that failures did not get blown out of proportion. If that happened, it would inflict damage on the larger Reliance group, in terms of its equity stock prices and external image, and dent the 'big guys' image. Traditionally, there has been an unfair expectation in capital markets that Reliance would always do business on a big format and succeed at it. The company was expected to be invincible, much like the hero in many Indian movies. Otherwise, fans of the hero would not like the movie and it would flop miserably.

We continued to follow the principles of keeping a low profile and letting our work speak for itself. It takes time for the naive to find a voice. This comes through achievement, not through announcements and lack of effort.

BEYOND VALUE OF DOCUMENTS

Reliance Life Sciences has had its share of unwise decisions that may seem silly to individuals experienced in the business. But we should not forget that the best of company managers have made fundamental errors of judgement. An elephant can also slip and fall, goes an old Indian saying.

But through experience, Reliance Life Sciences has accumulated intellectual capital. It is important to capture intellectual capital in every way that it can be harnessed. This is for the benefit of future managers in the company. One way to capture it is through standard operating procedures, manuals, documents, presentations, reports, communications…which collectively have significant value. This book is a way of sharing intellectual capital that would be useful to external audiences, and to budding entrepreneurs and students of management.

But documents have limitations. Let's say you give a fairly well-trained team a bunch of documents pertaining to biopharmaceutical filling operations. Then ask them to do filling operations for a few batches. In all likelihood, the operations will have several issues since this know-how is accumulated from years of collective experience. No value can be assigned to this experience.

An example of a Turkish company comes to my mind. In January 2015, we were in Istanbul negotiating a licensing agreement for a monoclonal antibody. The Turkish company wanted to buy only the drug substance from us and do the filling and finishing operations in Turkey. We had no issues with this. However, during negotiations, they were unwilling to pay when it came to compensating Reliance Life Sciences personnel for onsite support during the actual filling operations in Turkey. We would have none of this. They were not assigning any value to our qualified, trained and experienced human resources. Not to speak of the opportunity costs involved in our operations managers spending time at the facility in Turkey at the cost of work in Navi Mumbai. Their position also conveyed a sense that Indian managers can be hired for a song, given that the same company would have paid thousands of dollars to a western country for its human resources. Not surprisingly, this term in the contract was a deal-breaker and we walked out.

LEARNING IS RELATIVE

The learning from building Reliance Life Sciences is no different. It is a reference point that others can gain insights from. But variability brought about by the context of strategy, sector, company, customers, linkages, country, competency... must be factored in before application. Learning from Reliance

Life Sciences is also time- and period-dependent and depends on investor and management mindsets, evolutionary state, markets, science and technology context, and intellectual property environment.

However, there are several underlying lessons. But the resident knowledge and know-how in the minds of the key creators can never be fully brought out, given the limitations of memory, extent of detail, expressions and an enabling environment that supports shared learning. Science and technology have not even scratched the surface of mankind's understanding about the human brain.

IGNORANCE IS BLISS

What is striking is the innocence of many of us who set out to build the Reliance Life Sciences initiative. From one perspective, this was a positive factor, because it led us to learn about, and experiment with, opportunities without knowing what would be in store for us. From another perspective, it was foolish to venture into a relatively unknown space. A Silicon Valley venture capitalist, after I had taken him through a presentation on our initiative in the early part of our evolution, sarcastically said, 'Good luck to you and your investors.' With that, the meeting ended. I had met him not to seek investment, but at the instance of a third person in the industry.

TRUST MOTIVATES

But we were in a state of bliss and continued on our path. What mattered to us was the trust that Mukesh Ambani placed in the biotechnology initiative and in our abilities. However, we had to live up to this trust and prove that we were worthy. This was undoubtedly a great motivating factor. It became a rallying point for the core leadership, and continues to be so, to this day.

Come to think of it, trust can be a big motivator for performance, behaviour and integrity. Many employees had faith and trust in Reliance. So did their family members, vendors, customers, business partners, regulators and many other stakeholders. Consequently, the stress levels on the core leadership multiplied. We could not fail and this created stress.

INTERNALIZE BUSINESS

The emotive connect with the enterprise made us live and breathe the business. It was not a dream, but a possibility that was dependent on our collective intellect and actions. We had to think, plan and move relentlessly hour after hour, day after day and month after month. There was no respite. Our future was tied to the business. So were our aspirations, and our quality of life and that of our families. In turn, the future of the business was tied to us.

Reliance Life Sciences is integral to me and to several members of the core leadership and their families. To be successful in business you have to think and relate to it round the clock, 365 days a year. It goes beyond a professional engagement. It has to be ingrained in your genes. The stakes for us were far too high. Failure would make us faceless. Success would be just one more stride.

NOTHING VENTURED, NOTHING GAINED

So goes the adage. Except that, in our case, the venture was a voyage. We had to act to make progress. We had to do so in order to learn. We could not be tethered to our past, but had to live in the present and seek the future. There was no time to bask in past glory. The future was constantly beckoning. We ventured forward and even now, we are constantly moving, looking for opportunities. It has been a ceaseless pursuit. We have had to frequently realign or renew strategies and, in the process, swallow our pride. Sometimes, we smart from matters that do not materialize, at other times, we are radiant because of a win that we worked hard for.

FALLS HELP TO RISE AND FOCUS

We have had our share of falls. They became touchpoints with ground reality. But we could not sit idle and lament after a fall. We had to recover, rise and run to make up for lost time and the additional costs. The focus had to be on the goals of growth, profitability, sustainability and social good. Our falls taught us about the inherent fallacies and pitfalls in losing focus. A good footballer never loses sight of the ball even as he or she dives or falls. Likewise, a good baseball or a cricket player never takes his eye off the ball till it is time for a new delivery.

Mukesh Ambani constantly goaded us into focusing. He would have little time to listen to us and would have little empathy for our multiple engagements. Once, during a one-on-one meeting he asked me why I was not flagging the severe problems that I faced. I replied that he had far more problems to worry about and that I would do everything within my abilities to solve the problems of Reliance Life Sciences, instead of burdening him. He did not say anything. In leadership, setbacks are bound to happen. There is no point in saying we made a mistake or faced an issue, without first getting into a mindset to remedy and move ahead. That's why we are in leadership.

In one of our lyophilization cycles for tissue plasminogen activator, in the final stage of the process, the vials inside the machine came out broken. All parameters were checked and found to be fine. It was a big disappointment, given the large value of the batch and missed schedules. It was like a baby being stillborn. However, this loss did not deter us. We carried out a detailed investigation, traced the problem to the packing configuration of half-bunged vials laid out in trays and placed in the machine for lyophilization.

Then, there are the naysayers, postulating pessimists or those who themselves feel threatened. They exaggerate the dangers but don't offer solutions. Their job is to say 'I said so', when there is a setback. Our job is to carry on, regardless.

RECONFIGURE IF REQUIRED

There are times when a business has to be reconfigured. Such a call for action is due to several factors, ranging from market, technology, industry, economy, mergers and acquisitions, taxation, public policies and leadership. Reliance Life Sciences had a situation in its pharmaceutical initiative when a relatively large budget was approved for a generic, small molecule business. In 2008, the global financial meltdown happened. All major projects across the Reliance group were critically reviewed to reduce capital exposure and conserve cash. The pharmaceutical business had additional issues of a laterally inducted leadership being disconnected from operating principles and corporate governance standards. It naturally got the merciless axe which it deserved.

I had the undertaker's task. Along with Rahul Padhye in corporate development and well-meaning colleagues in the pharmaceutical team, we reconfigured the business to keep it small to begin with. We focused it on a differentiated set of products in the oncology domain. This met with approval and the business is now gaining traction under the leadership of Santhosh Mathai.

RIGIDITY STIFLES

In almost all cases of creation, there is a vast difference between the original ideation or imagination, and the final result. During the creative process, some aspects may be mutated or may not be to the creator's liking. However, there is no place for rigidity in the creative process and it is important to remember that no creation is complete or forever. It is a continuum. What Reliance Life Sciences created is very different from what it set out to do, in the first place. The life sciences campus in Navi Mumbai is an example. We had provided two floors, each with 30,000 sq. ft. area, with rooms for contract research for customers. However, the business was not easily forthcoming and two of the floors were converted to a plasma fractions-to-finished products manufacturing and dedicated fill-finish facility. A large and expansive pharmaceutical project was reconfigured to a much smaller one in the Navi Mumbai campus. Its business model was changed to new generation oncology products; complete from active pharmaceutical intermediates to oral dosage and injectable formulations with dedicated fill-finish and packing. A plant tissue culture facility was transformed to multiple and segregated areas for documentation, as well as a rabbit pyrogen testing facility for plasma protein products.

IGNORANCE IS NOT ALWAYS BLISS

Reliance Life Sciences was a novice when it set out to build its manufacturing facility. Our lack of experience and ignorance was not a complete disadvantage. It served us well in one context, but in another context, we got it all wrong. The first case is of the plasma proteins manufacturing facility. We had made the right call. We started a small manufacturing facility that did not cost much in capital expenditure and helped us take graduated steps and learn. We then bought a second-hand larger plant of the Red Cross in Finland which involved travelling to Finland at the height of winter. We did not know exactly what lay in store, and struggled initially to get the facility up and running. Soon enough, we had a scalable and viable business only limited by raw material availability.

The second case pertained to biopharmaceutical manufacturing. Here, we engaged a US-based international engineering consulting company, Aker Kvaerner, which designed a large facility for us in 2006. The facility was too big for us and cost a bomb.

DISPASSIONATE VIEWS

If you take a dispassionate view of a biological clean room facility, it is nothing but several large cold boxes placed adjacent to each other, with defined flows of people, material and waste. It, however, has to conform to very high standards of cleanliness, particle counts, sterility, temperature, humidity, air pressure and air flow. A biological or engineering professional would not like this simplistic perspective.

With this perspective gained, Reliance Life Sciences made a sea change in its project conceptualization and implementation strategy by banking on in-house teams and being aggressive in value engineering, without compromising on quality and regulatory compliance. In this way, we built very competitive facilities in a capital-intensive industry. This shift was important in our industry where capital charges made up a big proportion of total costs.

SPACE TO GROW

My father had four children to provide for—my sister, us twins and our younger brother. In addition, he had to support his aged parents and, at times of need, some members of the larger family. So he would have bigger shirts, pants and other clothes stitched for us twins, so that we did not outgrow them quickly; often the same material, colour and design of shirts and pants. My brother and I shared school textbooks, which had been passed down by our elder sister. Our unfortunate younger brother, at times, had to make do with our clothes and the same textbooks which, by the time they reached him, were badly dog-eared.

When I narrate these experiences from my childhood to my son and other youngsters, they are amused. But this thriftiness was required since resources were either limited or scarce and/ or money was hard to come by. We never protested about what our father gave us. Try doing this today with your children and you will have a riot at home. Talk about this in society and you will be treated with scorn.

This thrifty attitude was required when building Reliance Life Sciences. In the growth phase, Reliance Life Sciences was able to quickly develop facilities at a competitive cost, consistent with business requirements. We created spaces in the campus, not just land but also the shell structures of two buildings, for future expansion. In this way, we minimized cash burn and avoided having a messy site on which the foundation and superstructure would be created in future. The shell structures of the two buildings were an eyesore but served as a reminder for us to grow and expand. It was as if the buildings were pleading to us to give them an identity. Today, these two buildings have turned out to be a blessing. They have given us plenty of latitude and saved us a lot of time. We did not have to scurry around or waste time for land acquisition. In every new building that we built, we had entire floors or spaces kept free, so as to provide for expansion at relatively short notice.

During my petrochemical years, I learnt that it is relatively better to build a new facility as compared to expand or retrofit an existing one. This aspect is particularly relevant in the context of life sciences manufacturing facilities, which necessitate regulatory approvals at different stages, equipment qualification, area qualification, facility validation, three media fills to scale-up, exhibit batches and stability studies. So we kept extra space to create entirely new facilities at competitive costs, and were able to do this fast.

PROBLEM IN ONE'S BACKYARD

Unlike the extra space we kept for building facilities in the future, we could not keep extra machines or people. Machines could not be kept idle because of the high costs to maintain them in working condition, free from dust and moisture. Likewise, employees could not be kept idle. 'An idle mind is a devil's workshop', goes the saying. For us, an idle mind is like cancer. It can spread wrong ideas and negative energy very quickly.

But the common demand in Reliance Life Sciences was, 'We need more people.' This came more from senior leaders who had earlier worked for companies with large resources. The Reliance response was always, 'Show me that the position you want to hire will have productive work for eight to ten hours a day.'

In India, many business and functional heads falsely believe that employees do not cost much. They do not generally worry about productivity, and having more employees in the team is seen as a solution to many issues, when in fact, the problem lies elsewhere. In most cases, business and functional heads tend to blame everyone else, except themselves. But, often the problem is actually in their backyard. Either it is below their line of sight, or they do not want to see it and accept it. This is a mindset issue.

It is important for all companies to constantly focus on the productivity of their people, machines, facilities and finances. This is particularly relevant for companies in a startup and growth mode, when resources are hard to come by or are under strain.

THE SOAP IS ON

Once we had a situation where our recombinant protein manufacturing facility was in the commissioning phase.

A recently hired expatriate colleague raised the need for additional finances for completion. I was naturally not pleased. I dug my heels in on the premise that this should have been thought through much earlier. It so happened that Mukesh Ambani had come over to the life sciences site to inaugurate our annual employee event 'ReliFest'. As expected, he wanted a review. At the meeting, the issue of additional finances for the recombinant manufacturing facility was flagged to him by the expatriate colleague. I presented my viewpoint that this should have been thought through during detailing. Mukesh Ambani then told me in Hindi, *'Sabun to Lag Gaya'* or 'Soap has already been applied'. I could not understand his comment and had a confused look.

He then explained what he meant in English: While having a shower, if you have applied soap all over your body and the water flow stops (not unusual in India), you have no choice but to wait till the water supply is restored to complete your shower. Similarly, when you are deep into a project's execution phase, some additional capital expenditure, even if not originally envisaged, cannot be avoided. You have no choice but to spend the additional amount needed. It is well worth it to spend more money and get the project completed, as long as the amount is not much.

When a project is well underway and far beyond the point of no return, one should not mind incremental expenses. It is imperative that the project be completed, commissioned and operated. Otherwise the opportunity costs would be significant. This does not mean that project managers can assume 'the soap is on' and demand funding. There has to be merit in the additional expense, and it should go beyond the original plan.

WATCH OUT FOR THE TRIGGER HAPPY

When you are building a business, you are not only conceptualizing, creating the foundation, structure, superstructure, interiors, landscaping, and putting in place all the systems and processes, you are also building an ecosystem of human, environmental and cultural elements. Each one of these components is critical. In such a setting, there will be many different types of individuals, some of whom may either need to be corrected or jettisoned, because they tend to vitiate the atmosphere.

Reactive individuals are those who pull the trigger all of a sudden, or make allegations without understanding the details or what the real perspectives are. They quickly come to conclusions or draw premises, snap and fire like a machine gun. Their behaviour may affect other colleagues, causing the motivated ones to get demotivated, the 'stand-no-nonsense' ones to react with equal force, and the docile ones to feel helpless.

In such situations, the leadership has to step in and call for a truce. They can try to get the reactive person to see the other person's point of view, and see if there is any merit in the context. Following this, the leadership can get both sides to converge, based on a mature process of appreciating each other's point of view.

MOVE AT MY PACE

When you set a pace for development and growth, every member of the team, particularly those in the leadership team, have to work at the same pace and be on the same wavelength. A chain is only as strong as the weakest link. So organizations are as strong as the weakest team member. At the same time, you must provide for genuine individual shortcomings, arising out of personal and family issues and exigencies. You must also provide for genuine, non-controllable factors, particularly external factors, provided that there is sincerity of purpose and wholehearted effort.

As a leader you must be clear to set a pace that is much

more demanding on you than on the others in your team. If you want to adopt a leisurely pace, do not be surprised to see others moving at the same slow pace, or at an even slower pace. This can cause inertia to set in.

A leader has to set a fast pace for himself on programmes, projects, submissions and turnaround times. If some team members do not match this pace, the leader will need to give them an opportunity to catch up, after understanding their situation. And if this does not work, the leader will have to intervene appropriately.

WATCH OUT FOR THE SOCIETY-TYPES

Building a business also requires keeping certain types of people, such as society types, at arm's length. These people will act as if they have found a long-lost friend when they meet you and will invariably drop names, saying 'When I was with x person', to impress you. Then, there are social media commentators who have an opinion on everything but will never put in the hard work and relentless pursuit required for the task. Finally, there are media persons who have come to subconsciously believe that their lives revolve around picking on the shortfalls of others and seeking what is sensational; the word 'development' is not in their lingua franca. It is best that these people are ignored.

KICK THE HUMPTY DUMPTY OFF THE WALL

Then, there are the fence-sitters. These individuals are good at advising you on how the game should be played, but would never come on the field, roll up their sleeves, play and score goals. They often criticize and typically, have big egos. This group comprises of armchair managers, people with powers but no responsibility and accountability, and the make-believe do-gooders. It also includes some team members who keep talking about how things were in their previous company, instead of living within their current company context. These people are better taken off the wall, for they tend to get dysfunctional.

REMOVE THOSE BLINKERS

Many people are conditioned to think in a certain way, based on their upbringing, education and work and life experiences. Conditioned thinking can be dangerous, because there is a tendency to see things the way you are conditioned to see them. These people are like horses that always look forward due to the blinders or blinkers placed on the sides of their eyes. Their perspective tends to be limited.

At Reliance Life Sciences, we have had and continue to have, many individuals who think in a conditioned way. A biologist sees biology in everything, a chemist sees chemistry, an expert in High Pressure Liquid Chromatography (HPLC) only thinks of HPLC... Not many individuals of this type see a different view, a different angle of the same view or have a completely different perspective.

Unfortunately for the conditioned thinkers, innovation happens at the intersection of two disciplines; as very different as music and brain science, mathematics and genetics, biology and chemistry, management and irrationality, and so on. Likewise, solutions often lie in other domains.

Thinking in a conditioned way also disables conceptual and first principles' thinking. In one instance, we had issues with a bellow in an isolator system, in the liquid filling line for oncology products. The bellow used to frequently tear and cause air leaks, bringing production to a halt. The bellow was fabricated with a different material, which could not stand the stress of repeated mechanical motion in two dimensions. It had to push high-efficiency particulate filtered air without external air ingress, into the isolator. I suggested thinking from first principles on what an alternative bellow design could be, and had alternatives for the bellow material. At first I was brushed off by the engineering head. To his credit, he went back and thought deeply about the matter and came to me the same evening with a solution of silicon coating Tyvek fabric, to locally make a bellow. It worked well and we could afford to keep a couple of them as spares, thus having a very low downtime due to air ingress. There are many other examples of lateral thinking in Reliance Life Sciences.

DEMAND PERFORMANCE

At the end of it all, performance matters. Achievement matters more than effort. Finished goods matter more than work-in-process. Sales matter more than inventory. Collections matter more than sales revenues. Profits matter more than collections. Cash flows matter more than profits. Customer satisfaction matters more than cash flows.

For example, the satisfaction derived from developing a thrombolytic product that saves a heart attack patient from death gives immense satisfaction to my colleagues in the value chain, from molecular biology, process development, pre-clinical studies, clinical development, manufacturing, regulatory and support functions to marketing. In essence, the chain extends from ideation, innovation and implementation, to infusion into the patient in hospital.

WRONG ATTITUDE IS LIKE CANCER

Cancer is not just a biological phenomenon. It is an organizational, societal, national and global phenomenon as well. People who fall in this category include disgruntled employees, cynics, the financially corrupt, the morally corrupt, tax dodgers, unethical professionals, anti-social elements, rapists, sodomists, pseudo-secularists, fundamentalists, forced religious conversion missionaries, and terrorists. The degree of activity and harm varies. While, there is no one who is absolutely good, and all of us think negatively on and off, good thoughts have to overcome bad thoughts. And do-gooders have to unseat the bad guys.

At Reliance Life Sciences, we do not tolerate employees with a poor work attitude, people who make value judgements based on 'feelings', and people who believe that an activity will be of no use without actually evaluating it. One common refrain that I have heard from some colleagues, is about the project not being feasible or doable, without taking either time or effort to collectively think through its technical, commercial, organizational and financial feasibility.

EMPATHY FOR PEOPLE STIMULATES PERFORMANCE

In India, as well as in many other parts of the world, employees, their career aspirations and, their family's aspirations get intertwined with the organization's development and growth performance. Social status is a function of where one works, the nature of work, the level of responsibility and the compensation.

Many benefits and perquisites come with the position in government and quasi-government departments and in the organized private sector. This is not the case in the unorganized or informal sectors of the economy. Retirement or job losses can wipe away these benefits. Transfers and changes in location, can also wipe away benefits such as a good school for children, and employment for one's spouse. Retrenchment leads to a serious loss of face for the person in his or her larger family context, given that Indian society is yet to appreciate that job losses do take place and is not reflective of the person's capability.

The daily grind and hardships of life in cities, towns and villages, make many employees develop a steely resolve to overcome difficulties in their quest for good work, career and quality of life. The company plays an important role in the broader family and social context. As a result, employees tolerate adverse organizational situations, negativity emanating from the culture and some difficult bosses. This is until matters come to a breaking point.

Therefore, good leadership must have empathy, not sympathy, for the individual and family situation of every team member. People-related decisions taken must be sensitive to the context of the person(s) concerned. Such an approach helps motivate the person to give the very best to his leader and the organization.

SPEED ALONE DOES NOT THRILL

Decision-making in quick time is important but timing alone does not matter. What is needed are quick decisions combined with reasonable accuracy. This combination drives the agility of an organization. Most often, when more than one entity is involved, the least common denomination principle comes into play. The slower entity determines the pace. But market opportunities do not wait.

Some leadership members act quickly, but shoot from the hip. Like 'quick gun murugans', the Indian species of cowboys. Then there are those who get things right but move at a snail's pace. There are many who neither act quickly nor get it right. They have no place in organizations, least of all in leadership.

Very rarely does one come across leaders who act fast with reasonable accuracy. These individuals make it to the top because they are able to capitalize on opportunities and nip problems in the bud. A good part of this skill comes through experience and operating on principles. Most of the time, instinct, passion and hard-nosed perspectives come into play. When these leaders falter, they are quick to either withdraw or correct themselves, and move on without letting the grass grow under their feet.

Intensive and regular monitoring of payments is a must for any organization to succeed. At the marketing team level, it has to be on a daily basis. Imagine selling a product that you have toiled hard to research, develop and market, and your customers use it but do not pay for it. Have you not been made a fool of? So, why have mercy on such people? Money is indeed honey.

In business, you encounter many such companies and individuals who do not pay in time. A lot of management time and effort goes into chasing payments. Frustrations and frictions arise. Nothing new about this, but most companies make these mistakes; so did we.

It is understandable if a company is going through a difficult situation, and is making every effort to alleviate its payments position. We have had unpleasant experiences with several big Indian pharmaceutical companies that have hundreds of millions of dollars of surplus cash, endlessly delaying payments. The experience with some transnational companies has not been any better. They take gullible individuals, companies and banks for a ride.

In the Indian context, which neither has a legal system to ensure prompt payments, nor a national credit rating score system maintained by a credible independent agency, such characters have a free ride. Even those who manage to sustain a judicial case on bounced cheques and are able to get, after a long ordeal, an arrest warrant against the accused, may find that it is not enforced. The police are least interested in chasing and arresting individuals in cheque-bouncing cases. They claim to be understaffed and have bigger crimes to deal with. They are also preoccupied by matters of security for very important persons (VIP)—the culture of pampering VIPs in India is strong and stifling.

It's best to have a clear policy of 'show me the money' that calls for advance payments, or payments against irrevocable letters of credit, confirmed by international banks of repute. You are better off getting cash for products and services sold. It is also fine to have a system of prepaid cheques that are automatically deposited on the day or the next day of despatch of materials. Only in very rare cases should credit be given, preferably backed by a strong payment track record. This is equally applicable to Indian and many overseas markets. The best experience that Reliance Life Sciences has had is with the UK, where companies pay very promptly once a contract is in place.

Without proper systems and processes, working capital that is locked with debtors, typically at high rates of interest, increases. Thus the costs add up. Most companies with high working capital to net turnover ratios have the inherent potential to unleash funds from within when inventory levels are reduced and a tight credit policy is followed.

TIME AND TIDE WAIT FOR NO MAN

This has been my favourite saying since my childhood days. Research experiments, technology developments, opportunities, customers, competitors, markets, prospective candidates...nobody, not even your boss, will wait for you. You have to determine your pace based on what the situation warrants, not what you are comfortable with, and deliver.

Most often, when Mukesh Ambani wanted a task to be accomplished, we would either get a sense of when he would want it completed, or I would ask him. Then, I would make every effort to get it done to his satisfaction, by that deadline. A consistent performer works in the same way and puts in the same effort, irrespective of the boss or organization he is working for. However, at times, it helps to ask the other person when he or she wants the job done. Apart from the positive customer experience that this question will trigger, it will help you set a personal deadline for the job you are trusted with. For example, when dealing with media personnel, it is useful to ask for their deadline. Once a commitment is made, it has to be honoured.

Unless you have this spirit, it is very difficult to get projects completed, pricing decisions made, products launched, customer complaints addressed, annual reviews completed... Imagine a world where timelines did not matter and everyone was left guessing. You wouldn't know when trains or planes left or when your food order would be delivered. Need I say more?

FRUSTRATIONS LINGER

As your research-driven products get commercialised, frustrations tend to rise, stemming from the infirmities in the drug and other regulatory systems in India and the ugly face of competition.

Regulatory system frustrations range from delays in approvals, rejection on illogical grounds, u-turns in decisions, dealing with egos and superegos and being a victim of cross-fire between different government departments and doctor's camps. In clinical studies, if the chief investigator is a doctor from one camp and the reviewer is from a rival camp...God help you!

For example, one subject expert committee on oncology had approved a biosimilar for a phase 1 clinical trial to support product registration overseas for exports, although a limited phase 3 clinical study was concurrently in progress for registration in India. In contrast, just a week later, another committee on nephrology rejected a phase 1 study proposal on another biosimilar, for product registration for exports, on the grounds that an India study was in progress and Indians cannot be treated as guinea pigs. So much for consistency!

The logic of Indians being guinea pigs is hard to relate to. India wants the benefits of new drugs, but wants the guinea pigs to be citizens from other nations. Strange! Undoubtedly, there have been inappropriate clinical studies done on unsuspecting Indian subjects. But if you look carefully, you will find that these have mostly been done by multinational companies. And many of these companies never paid compensation for deaths during the clinical trials.

The classic case is a vaccine study done by two transnationals—one American and the other British—on unsuspecting tribal children. Social activists took umbrage. Parliamentarians took up the activists' cause. The Ministry of Health came under pressure. Many new drug advisory committees in different medical domains were formed, and these were overseen by a technical committee and an apex committee. In the name of regulatory scrutiny, the clinical research industry was forced into morbidity.

For us at Reliance Life Sciences, having the national drug pricing authority fix the price of two biologicals on illogical grounds was frustrating. For over a year, we flagged this issue, met several officials and wrote memos to them. Finally, a senior official told us that the pricing issue was sorted out and the official order would be issued. The following week, when we met his boss, he asked who had told us that the pricing issue was sorted out. He said it was better for us to have the two products differentiated in the revised list of the National List of Essential Medicines. We were speechless.

At the Indian Institute of Management, Ahmedabad, I had taken a course on 'Legal Aspects of Business.' The course professor, who had an excellent sense of humour, used to tell us, 'Love and law have no logic.' Those words resounded in my mind and I mentioned them to the official from the drug pricing authority. Believe it or not, he readily agreed with me!

Market frustrations are easier to handle. Here again, the established transnational companies play havoc; not by themselves, but through distributors who are paid hefty commissions. Getting specifications tailored to their product, getting tender committees to reject others on silly technical grounds, pricing to prey on us as new entrants, taking care of doctors through overseas sponsored trips in the guise of seminars and medical education...these are old tricks, easily seen and addressed.

As a result, frustrations are the order of the day as you grow an organization. Dealing with frustrations needs resolve and resilience. Resolve to overcome them and resilience to engage with them, not giving up till the very end.

ADAPTING TO GET BETTER AND BETTER

Reliance Life Sciences, like most evolving organizations, develops competence on an adaptive basis. Competence develops through acquiring know-how with practice over a long period of time. It cannot be captured by patents. Plasma proteins is one area where to succeed, what matters is know-how. Learning by doing and getting better and better at it. A bunch of standard operating procedures is of very limited value. This is because, the Cohn's fractionation process, which is used for manufacturing plasma proteins, is not patented, but requires a certain know-how to practice.

But adaptive competence is much more than know-how. It's about having the ability to learn from adapting to environments and developments while keeping first principles in focus. Some part of it is generic across companies, and the larger part is context-specific. The know-how comes through developing adaptive competence. Conforming to far more demanding standards in manufacturing, such as of USFDA or the European Medicines Agency, is an example. The environment demands data integrity, transparency and traceability, as well as capture of out-of-specifications events and their in-depth investigations. Moving from one environment of quality standard to a better one requires new learning, new ways of doing things, institutionalizing them across the organization and ingraining them into the mindset.

In another context, there are several elements in nature that reflect adaptive competency. One is adaptive immunity, e.g. the human body develops immunity by adapting to antigens. In the context of business organizations, adaptive competence can be developed or destroyed. When a board decides to change management in one stroke, the adaptive competence of the organization goes for a toss. Such changes could be due to the board being disappointed with performance, external developments demanding a purge, chemistry and wavelength not matching between the board and management, unethical practices in vogue, political compulsions dictating a flush, or simply dislike of the management.

We saw this happening with an international biopharmaceutical company that is a contract manufacturing client. It had three successive cleansings of the top management which entailed that the company had to go through a learning process every time. During repeated management change, relationships with constituencies go down the drain. The problem gets compounded when the new management team has a cowboy attitude—a know-all, intellectually arrogant attitude, denouncing everything that the preceding management has done. Not many companies realize that in shooting from the hip, the management becomes a sitting duck.

Then, there are several manifestations of adaptive competence. Some examples are translating creativity and innovation into useful technologies, manufacturability, fine-tuned operations to meet stringent quality standards, achieving and sustaining high quality and scalability of business.

LETTING GO OF ADAPTIVE COMPETENCE

The process of letting go inherently involves letting go of adaptive competence in the leader or the group. However, this can be largely, not absolutely, prevented by enlightened succession and institutionalizing organizational learning. This is what I have strived to do at Reliance Life Sciences through developing leadership, institutionalizing systems and processes, involving larger teams in reviews and, in recent years, moving to delegating based on a framework.

IT'S A LONG HAUL

At the end, it is a long haul, more so in a capital intensive, research, development and talent driven, long gestation business in a highly regulated environment. Opportunities abound. In biotechnology, unmet medical needs revolve around novel proteins, competitively-priced products of global quality, and products that often see short supply, particularly in developing countries.

The way to engage with such an industry is to make every effort to address market needs. Constantly keep profitable market entry in focus. Be expansive in engagement in the product-market arena. Recognize new opportunities in a given product-market domain, through new products, new geographies, new medical indications of use, the unaddressed socio-economic profile of patients and later generation products and services. The deeper a product portfolio is and the wider the market participation is, the better the ability to grow the business consistently and sustainably. All this should be done without losing sight of capital cost, exposure to debt and risk management.

14

WORKING WITH PRINCIPLES

'Latitude to perform renders
expansiveness to a business.'

Embracing principles facilitates orderly growth and development. Principles help shape the organization and manage it. Some principles stem from an individual's upbringing. Others from the organization's psyche. Yet others come the hard way from action learning.

Principles are normally spelt out for guidance, with some latitude for the context and bona fide mistakes. They are not cast in stone, but evolve based on collective experiences and the need to adapt to changing times.

In building Reliance Life Sciences and facilitating its growth and development, I have come to embrace some principles. With several parallel research programmes, projects, manufacturing facilities, clinical trials, product launches, partnerships and people involved, it was important to enunciate principles within a managing framework.

I have been exposed to some of these principles through my upbringing and my past professional engagements. Other principles have come about through learning the hard way from the process of evolution of Reliance Life Sciences. So, what are these principles? Nothing complicated. Just a basic set. These are not prescriptions for performance. At best, they can provide some learning. Take them in part or in full; or leave them.

SET PRINCIPLES. GIVE LATITUDE.

Manage by articulating a clear set of guiding principles. Give latitude for performance, mistakes and odd behaviour at times. In the early stage of development, you can micro-manage up to a point. But once the organization gets into gear and you have a good sense of the calibre of the leadership team, you must let them decide within a framework that you spell out.

LATITUDE IS NOT THE SAME AS FREEDOM

Latitude provides a degree of freedom within an organization's stated objectives and guidelines. Freedom depends on the boundaries set by you. Reliance Life Sciences had the latitude to decide for itself. But it had to conform to the larger Reliance group's polices. It could not expect to have the complete freedom to do what it liked to do, because, in any context, unbridled freedom is a utopian concept. At the same time, Reliance Life Sciences had empowerment, which is about confidence that any criteria-based decision taken in the organization's interest would be backed by Mukesh Ambani.

WHEN IN A DILEMMA, ASK WHAT IS IN THE INTEREST OF THE CUSTOMER AND THE COMPANY

You will invariably come to the right decision. This principle is relevant to companies as much as it is to families. The customer can be internal or external. The organizational unit can be the company or the family.

GET CARRIED AWAY BY SCALE AT YOUR RISK

A high scale of operations is good for growth, costs and competitive advantage, but not when the chips are down. The downside is very damaging and will overshadow the benefits. Manufacturing at high scale is fine, but you have to be paranoid about the very high cost of batch failures. So, scale up in a graduated way, but with flexibility of formats. Ramping up on people is great, but if the chaff is not separated from the wheat, in an adverse situation, you will be left with the chaff and, consequently, operational issues and low human productivity.

SEE THE INFIRM IN INTEGRATION

Integration makes good corporate strategic sense. When there is stress induced by markets or operations, the weak link has the ability to damage the strong links as well, causing the chain to lose strength. In a highly interdependent operation like plasma proteins manufacture, non-performance by a small element in the integration—equipment, on-line parameter measurements and offline quality testing—can wreak havoc, given that proteins are very sensitive.

CONFINES CAN GET YOU INTO CHAINS

When people limit their thinking and ability to their own context and competence, they become prisoners of their minds. When such individuals are part of a team, you get the least common denominator in team performance. What matters more are the larger company imperatives. There came a stage in our evolution when we could not remain prisoners of our own abilities in research, development, manufacturing and marketing. We had to outsource, whether through a licence or partnership.

CONDITIONED THINKING LEAVES YOU WITH TUNNEL VISION

Most people think, extrapolate and come to conclusions based on the way they have been brought up and taught, or what they have experienced. To drive innovation, drive performance and manage people, you and your team members need to break free from thinking anchored in the past. For instance, after thinking in the same frame when we were struggling to get a lyophilization cycle for a recombinant protein right, we sought help from an academician. He thought differently and had a solution in good time.

DON'T TAKE NO FOR AN ANSWER

There are many individuals who are quick to say 'No' or 'Not possible'. Tell them and show them how it is possible. Sooner or later they will come around. Many people tend to take soft options or walk away from resolving a problem. But when you insist, they invariably find a way.

TOLERATE IMPERFECTION, BUT NOT BAD ATTITUDES

A bad attitude is like cancer. It grows, mutates and spreads. Cut it out when its first signs are visible.

READ. MEET. INTERACT. LISTEN

Be prolific in your reading. Read anything related to your subject and about the industry, science, technology, society and the world that you can lay your hands on. Meet people and interact with them. A large part of learning comes from interacting with others and being attentive. I was uninitiated in biology, but had a resolve to learn and did so through these methods.

SHOW EMPATHY, NOT SYMPATHY

Empathy puts you in a solution-oriented mindset. Sympathy tends to cloud your judgement. When you have to ask a team member to leave for poor performance, you can empathize with his situation. However, if you sympathize, you may find it hard to let the person go.

NEVER REGRET YOUR DECISIONS

Decisions are made in a context, maybe with incomplete or imperfect information, and based on the state of evolution and the aspirations of the individual or organization. Anybody can be wise in hindsight. At Reliance Life Sciences, we made a few wrong decisions but we never regretted them. Our approach was 'damage done, let's digest it and move on'.

DERIVE AMUSEMENT FROM OBSERVING

Have a keen eye for observing people wherever you go—from what they wear, how they behave, body language, stress levels, to what they do when they think nobody is observing them. This makes you see what others don't. It improves your insight, which you can apply with caution in many work and life situations.

WORK HARD, AS IF THERE IS NO TOMORROW. EARN YOUR FUN

At the end of it all, work very hard, as if there is no tomorrow. Earn your fun, only after having worked hard. Make it a point to celebrate every major achievement. Sleep like a log of wood. Be hyperactive when you are awake. At Reliance Life Sciences, the leadership team celebrates as one single group once in a year, typically on 1 April of each year, immediately after a financial year ending. We raise a toast. The next day, it is back to the grind. Individual groups have small celebrations for almost every new accomplishment—marketing approval for a product, a plant's commissioning, a major deal, to name a few.

JOKE ABOUT YOURSELF FIRST BEFORE YOU JOKE ABOUT OTHERS

Finally, have the ability to laugh at yourself. It is a great trait. It helps relieve stress. So does joking about others, as along as it does not violate the sensitivity and personal space of an individual, community or country. You have no right to good-naturedly joke about others, unless you have the ability to joke about yourself, or be joked about.

15

ENVISIONING THE FUTURE

'Gateways abound for those who get into gear.'

Opportunities are boundless, but it is for the leadership to find opportunities and go about systematically and meticulously mapping out the opportunity domains, understand the product-market-medical context, detail manufacturing and technical feasibility, work out linkages, scope out facilities, spell out specific goals and objectives, chart the dimensions of the business components, work out the financial feasibility, tie-up funding, profile competencies required and, finally, detail an implementation plan.

FOUNDATION BUILT

Reliance Life Sciences has reached a position of high revenue growth, strong financials, a low level of bank borrowings, and a solid pipeline of products and services across several domains in biology and medicine. It employs competent people, has strong systems and processes and above all, has a work culture that is performance-oriented, consensus-driven, hands-on, and has a fun element as well. It has powerful engines of research and development, an array of programmes for developing several products within diverse domains and a robust marketing team.

Above all, in Reliance Life Sciences, there is collective involvement at the leadership level in building a strong future, and pride that the company is able to stand on its feet financially, and not be dependent on promoters' funding. Additionally, it has a strong balance sheet with the highest level of credit rating.

Reliance Life Sciences' leadership has the conviction that the width of biology-based products and services, currently marketed and under development, combined with a gradual increase in coverage of markets all over the world, is the basis for a higher rate of profitable and sustainable growth.

REINFORCING THE FOUNDATION

However, there are areas that need strengthening in Reliance Life Sciences. From a content perspective, there are prospects for unfolding opportunity domains that Reliance Life Sciences is currently engaged with—globalization of existing businesses, bio-betters, regenerative medicine-based therapies, molecular medicine-based advanced diagnostics, advanced wound management products, cosmetic surgery and novel proteins. From a management perspective, there are imperatives in improving depth of leadership, instituting advanced performance metrics, driving stronger market research, fostering ubiquitous technology applications in all spheres, making greater efforts in novel proteins, and enabling competencies to participate in partnerships in more developed markets.

Not that these areas were unattended to. They could not get the full attention they deserved at the different stages of the company's evolution. This was due to the compulsions of growth and concomitant issues related to its financial health, predictability of cash flows, technology, product development, marketing and leadership. This is a state which every new venture, new family relationship or new mission faces; a stage between settling down and building for greater accomplishments and achievements.

GOING FORWARD

Reliance Life Sciences is currently investing in additional manufacturing facilities with incremental investment. These investments leverage the brown-field status of the campus, which translates into cost benefits from using existing infrastructure for utilities, warehouses, quality testing laboratories and site management. In addition, there is a major benefit in the compressed timelines to get projects going, mechanically completed, commissioned, validated, and getting regulatory clearances and commercial manufacturing started.

Three years back, we were given freedom to make capital investments as long as we generated internal resources for funding them. So we have freedom within a well-defined framework. In 2013, we wrote a five-year corporate plan on our own initiative. I sent it to Mukesh Ambani. He studied every aspect of it and guided us through four revisions; from an asset-light model approach to an approach that entailed capital expenditure coming from internal resources, no borrowings and no compromise on revenue projections. The five-year corporate plan, with granularity for the first three years, sets both directions and specifics.

NEAR TERM AGENDA

The near term agenda will be about strengthening financials. For several years, cash profits have been generated on a sustained basis. Reliance Life Sciences has operational profitability and the ability to fund capital expenditure on its own. Consequently, it has had a much stronger balance sheet and the highest credit ratings for both short-term and long-term funding.

This situation will help Reliance Life Sciences invest in larger manufacturing facilities in the Navi Mumbai site. In the process, it will help it scale up to the next level, as more products come into play and newer markets open up following regulatory approvals.

This situation is very similar to that of a space mission, which demands an enormous amount of energy to take the payload into space, then substantially reduces fuel burn to manoeuver the spacecraft to the right trajectory and orbit.

MEDIUM TERM

In the medium term, there are opportunities for business expansion through new research and clinical development and commercial manufacturing facilities, in India or in another country with a strategic advantage.

In an aerospace context, the parallel is in attaining higher trajectories by bringing resources and manoeuverability skills into play, and deriving energy from the sun to drive systems.

LONG TERM

In the longer term, Reliance Life Sciences has the opportunity to monetize and globalize the business. This process will continue to be reinforced with more and more research-based, differentiated, hospital products entering the market. Equally it will be strengthened by an increasing number of product registrations in overseas markets.

Consequently, there are several potentially interesting ways to monetize and globalize Reliance Life Sciences. These range from going out on its own steam, forging a strategic partnership with equity stake in part or full, strategic alliances and participation in capital markets.

BEYOND

Beyond the long term lie opportunities in completely new but related domains—biomaterials for medical applications from marine sources, designer drugs, highly specific drugs for central nervous disorders, and so on. The boundary between beyond and yonder remains obscure. However, these engagements involve extending competencies in the existing domains and fostering new competencies.

It is best not to postulate or list imperatives. The inherent imponderables in the industry, in the discovery to development value chain, and the very long gestation periods involved, can limit a long-term perspective to a general road map. In the case of Reliance Life Sciences, this involves its superordinate goal and its timeless values.

The superordinate goal that drives Reliance life Sciences is to discover and develop solutions for unmet medical needs, primarily for the developing world. The timeless values enshrined in Reliance Life Sciences revolve around innovation-driven, high-quality, competitively-priced, differentiated products and services, consistently available in diverse medical domains.

As long as these two aspects of superordinate goals and values are part of the DNA of Reliance Life Sciences, it will continue creating value for its constituencies and society in general.

LARGER PERSPECTIVE

At Reliance Life Sciences, it is believed that what mankind has developed as biotechnology-based solutions to address medical needs, stems from one frontier that includes product groups, pathogen types, technology approaches and disease categories. Understanding the depth and diversity within each of these surface elements enables the discovery of solutions and their development. Fermentation products, peptides, antibody conjugates are some examples in context.

What Reliance Life Sciences has accomplished so far, as part of its evolution, is evidence of how it came from nowhere to create a biotechnology-based innovation platform to alleviate patient sufferings. Reinforcing its core engagements and enablers, and reaching out to the larger world offers it opportunities to have greater societal impact.

Science and technology are opening up new frontiers. There are several new domains, such as synthetic biology and marine biology which can be minefields of opportunities, once sufficient momentum has been built in the existing frontier.

CRYSTAL BALL GAZING

Biotechnology continues to be an evolving domain. Every day, new discoveries are being reported. In Mumbai, when I head out to work in the morning, I scan my emails on my mobile phone while sitting in my car, and unfailingly find an email sent to management team members by Dr Arnab Kapat, Director, Reliance Institute of Life Sciences. Typically, the email will have a report on a new science finding pertaining to cells, tissues, therapies, devices and nanotechnology.

It is important to recognize that most of these discoveries would take years, may be decades, to come into clinical practice. But what is amazing is the sheer magnitude of work that is going on across the world and the discoveries being made. What then are the boundaries of cell biology?

Imagine that you are lying on your stomach on a glass-bottomed boat on the surface of an ocean. Stare at its depths. There are hundreds of marine life forms out there, maybe millions and trillions at a microscopic level. They are diverse in their forms, shapes, ability to tolerate pressures, light and temperature, the way they breathe, survive and grow. What then are the boundaries of marine biology?

Now imagine that you are lying on your back on the ground facing a clear sky with all the stars near, far and distant. What lies there? Is there life yonder and beyond? How has all this been ordained and who has programmed it? What then are the boundaries of astrobiology?

Just three unexplored domains—cell biology, marine biology and astrobiology—tell us of the expanse of opportunity that biology offers. Mankind has some sense of what comes yonder and a vague sense of what comes beyond. But what lies beyond the yonder is in the realm of imagination. It is fascinating and mind-boggling. In every sense, it tells us how very little we know, and how much there is to discover. Generations are not enough to explore and fathom these mysteries which appear to be in the realm of science fiction.

But, sooner or later, fiction turns to facts and then to technology. Remember the movie *2001 A Space Odyssey*? I saw it first in the seventies when I was doing my engineering studies. I saw it once again in January 2015. I continue to be dumbfounded by it. Remember the television serial 'Star Trek'. I saw it in the eighties when I used to live in Baroda. Many of the concepts in the movie and the serial were then in the realm of imagination or fiction, but are real today. Or take the movie 'Martian', released in 2015, on how an understanding of science at a fundamental level can enable survival on an extremely hostile-to-life planet.

Naivety is universal. Getting a better sense is a quest. Humility lies in the acceptance of the eternal nature of knowledge.

EPILOGUE

A business is not inanimate. A CEO cannot be dispassionate. The business and the purpose of business have to be deeply rooted and genetically engineered. Find an end in human purpose and the business will unfold, evolve, grow and prosper. Science, research and technology are means to an end. Many can build a house, but few can create a home.

In the business of biotechnology, or for other businesses which alleviate human suffering, patents do not matter much, patients and citizens do. Affluence does not matter, affordability and access do. Personalities do not matter, passions and performance do. CEOs are transitory. Companies built on the edifice of humanity are enduring. A CEO's account is only of limited reference. The ability to imagine and implement is a testimonial.

In the context of life sciences, mankind has a very negligible understanding of this domain in relation to its seemingly unbounded expanse. Those who proclaim themselves as experts are as naive as they were at birth.

Building a successful company from scratch, like life, is a long haul. Aspirations take time to sink in and can change as the journey evolves. New beginnings are often made. Adjustments to new environments are required. New relationships and engagements get built while old ones may fade away or get discarded. Adaptive competence develops into leadership.

Quality of life, as with products and services, evolves as part of a journey and is not a destination. Success does not last long. Setbacks are soon overcome and fade in memory. New challenges and new excitements come up. What do not change are the imperatives of constant learning from the physical, spatial and intellectual worlds, as well as the timeless values that can inspire generations. Long-term success calls for a process of constant renewal and creative destruction.

When is birth and when is the end? Who knows? Where is the beginning and where is the end? Who cares? Who is the know-nothing and who is the know-all? Who understands? There are only postulations, philosophies, premonitions and prophecies. True knowledge is esoteric.

This portrayal of Reliance Life Sciences captures only one phase of a long haul. It is context-specific, but some broad lessons can be inferred—not as prescriptions but as pointers.

It has been a long journey from birth. The nurturing continues...and wings have enabled its flight.

ACKNOWLEDGEMENTS

The immense contribution of hundreds of my colleagues to the building and growth of Reliance Life Sciences. They placed their trust in me, responded to my often unreasonable demands, and worked shoulder-to-shoulder in building the foundation of Reliance Life Sciences, brick by brick. In doing so, they treated both achievements and frustrations as ephemeral.

The encouragement and support provided by Mukesh Ambani, Chairman and Managing Director, Reliance Industries Limited, which have been invaluable. In February 2014, I suggested to him that I would like to share my learning in building Reliance Life Sciences. He encouraged me to write this book.

The business exposure and insights into organizational ethos and cultural factors provided to me by Hasmukh Shah, former chairman of Indian Petrochemicals Corporation Limited (IPCL), which have been a treasure.

The value for resources and the high standards of propriety and conduct required for responsible positions that I learnt from the late Subrato Ganguly, former chairman and managing director of Indian Petrochemicals Corporation Limited (IPCL) and Engineers India Limited.

My wife Saroj, son Santosh and twin brother K.V. Balasubramaniam who helped me develop the resolve to write this book, and provided me valuable feedback.

My valued colleagues, Jamila Joseph and PV Raju; my good friends, Krishna Gopalan and Prof. Narasimhan Srinivasan who gave me inputs and assisted me in meticulously reviewing the draft. Narayanan Kutty from my office, facilitated my writing in the midst of demanding work commitments.

www.ingramcontent.com/pod-product-compliance
Lightning Source LLC
Chambersburg PA
CBHW022042210326
41458CB00080B/6535/J